First World War
and Army of Occupation
War Diary
France, Belgium and Germany

GUARDS DIVISION
1 Guards Brigade
Coldstream Guards
2 Battalion
1 August 1915 - 31 January 1919

WO95/1215/2

The Naval & Military Press Ltd
www.nmarchive.com
Published in association with The National Archives

Published by

The Naval & Military Press Ltd

Unit 10 Ridgewood Industrial Park,

Uckfield, East Sussex,

TN22 5QE England

Tel: +44 (0) 1825 749494

www.naval-military-press.com

www.nmarchive.com

This diary has been reprinted in facsimile from the original. Any imperfections are inevitably reproduced and the quality may fall short of modern type and cartographic standards.

© Crown Copyright
Images reproduced by permission of The National Archives, London, England, 2015.

Contents

Document type	Place/Title	Date From	Date To
Heading	BEF Guards Div Gds Bde 2 Bn Coldstream Guards 1915 Aug 1919 Jan From 2 Div 4 Bde		
Miscellaneous	Guards Div		
Heading	1st Guards Brigade Guards Division War Diary 2nd Battn. Coldstream Guards August 1915		
Miscellaneous	On His Majesty's Service.		
War Diary		01/08/1915	31/08/1915
Heading	1st Guards Brigade Guards Division War Diary 2nd Battn Coldstream Guards September 1915		
Miscellaneous	On His Majesty's Service.		
War Diary		01/09/1915	30/09/1915
Heading	1st Guards Brigade Guards Division War Diary 2nd Battn Coldstream Guards October 1915		
Miscellaneous	On His Majesty's Service.		
War Diary		01/10/1915	31/10/1915
Heading	1st Guards Brigade Guards Division War Diary 2nd Battn Coldstream Guards November 1915		
Miscellaneous	On His Majesty's Service.		
War Diary		01/11/1915	30/11/1915
Heading	1st Guards Brigade Guards Division War Diary 2nd Battn Coldstream Guards December 1915		
Miscellaneous	On His Majesty's Service.		
War Diary		01/12/1915	31/12/1915
Heading	1st Guards Brigade Guards Division 2nd Battalion Coldstream Guards January 1916		
Heading	2/Coldstream Gds Jan Vol XVI		
War Diary		01/01/1916	31/01/1916
Heading	1st Guards Brigade Guards Division 2nd Battalion Coldstream Guards February 1916		
Heading	2 Coldstream Gds Vol XVII		
War Diary	Pont Du Hem	01/02/1916	10/02/1916
War Diary	La Gorgue	11/02/1916	29/02/1916
Heading	1st Guards Brigade Guards Division 2nd Battalion Coldstream Guards March 1916		
Heading	2 Coldstream Gd Vol XVIII		
War Diary		01/03/1916	31/03/1916
Heading	1st Guards Brigade Guards Division 2nd Battalions Coldstream Guards April 1916		
Heading	2 Coldstream Gds Vol XIX		
War Diary		01/04/1916	30/04/1916
Heading	1st Guards Brigade Guards Division 2nd Battalion Coldstream Guards May 1916		
War Diary		01/05/1916	31/05/1916
Heading	1st Guards Brigade Guards Division 2nd Battalion Coldstream Guards June 1916		
War Diary		01/06/1916	30/06/1916
Heading	1st Guards Brigade Guards Division 2nd Battalion Coldstream Guards July 1916		
War Diary		01/07/1916	31/07/1916

Heading	1st Guards Brigade Guards Division 2nd Battalion Coldstream Guards August 1916		
War Diary		01/08/1916	31/08/1916
Heading	1st Guards Brigade Guards Division 2nd Battalion Coldstream Guards September 1916		
War Diary		01/09/1916	30/09/1916
Heading	1st Guards Brigade Guards Division 2nd Battalion Coldstream Guards October 1916		
War Diary		01/10/1916	31/10/1916
Heading	1st Guards Brigade Guards Division 2nd Battalion Coldstream Guards November 1916		
War Diary		01/11/1916	30/11/1916
Heading	1st Guards Brigade Guards Division 2nd Battalion Coldstream Guards December 1916		
War Diary		01/12/1916	28/02/1917
War Diary	In The Field	01/03/1917	31/07/1917
Miscellaneous	Appendix "A"		
Miscellaneous	2nd Battalion Coldstream Guards Report On The Operations		
War Diary	In The Field	01/08/1917	31/10/1917
Miscellaneous	Report On The Advance Over the Broenbeek Oct 9th-10th	12/10/1917	12/10/1917
War Diary	In The Field	01/11/1917	30/11/1917
Miscellaneous	2nd Battalion Coldstream Guards Account Of Operations	09/12/1917	09/12/1917
Miscellaneous	G.10/121	23/11/1917	23/11/1917
War Diary	In The Field	01/12/1917	31/12/1917
Miscellaneous	Honours & Awards		
War Diary	In The Field	01/02/1918	31/03/1918
Heading	Guards Division 1st Guards Brigade War Diary 2nd Battalion The Coldstream Guards April 1918		
War Diary		01/04/1918	12/04/1918
War Diary	In The Field	13/04/1918	31/05/1918
Miscellaneous	Account of Raid Carried Out On The Night Of The 22/23rd May 1918 By No 1 Company, 2nd Battalion Coldstream Guards	01/06/1918	01/06/1918
War Diary	In The Field	01/06/1918	28/08/1918
Miscellaneous	Account of Attack Made By The 2nd Battalion Coldstream Guards On The 27th August 1918	27/08/1918	27/08/1918
War Diary	In The Field	29/08/1918	30/09/1918
Miscellaneous	2nd Battalion Coldstream Guards Narrative Of Operations	01/10/1918	01/10/1918
Heading	1st Gds Bde Gds Div War Diary 2nd Bn Coldstream Guards October1918		
War Diary	In The Field	01/10/1918	31/10/1918
Miscellaneous	2nd Battalion Coldstream Guards Operations of 2nd Battalion Coldstream Guards		
Miscellaneous	2nd Battalion Coldstream Guards Narrative Of Operations		
War Diary	In The Field	01/11/1918	31/01/1919
Miscellaneous	2nd Battalion Coldstream Guards Narrative Of Operations	06/11/1918	06/11/1918

B.E.F.

GUARDS DIV.

Gds Bde.

2 Bn. Coldstream Guards.

1915 Aug - 1919 Jan

FROM 2 DIV 4 BDE

GUARDS DIV

45 San Sect

Box 889

To 2 ARMY

1st Guards Brigade.
Guards Division.

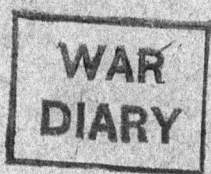

2nd BATTN. COLDSTREAM GUARDS.

A U G U S T

1 9 1 5

On His Majesty's Service.

346

Army Form C. 2118.

WAR DIARY
or
INTELLIGENCE SUMMARY.
(Erase heading not required.)

2nd Bn Coldstream Guards

Hour, Date, Place	Summary of Events and Information	Remarks and references to Appendices
1915.		
1st August	In Billets at Le Quesnoy	
2nd "	ditto	
3rd August	Bn. Bivouac at S. Inform and relieved 1st Bn Herts Regiment in Trenches B.3. Section Le Plantin.	
4th "	In Trenches. a quiet day. No casualties.	
5th "	" "	
5th August	Bn. relieved by 1st Bn Herts Regiment at Dark and returned to Billets at Le Quesnoy. In Billets at Le Quesnoy	
6th "	" "	
	Battalion bivouac at Dark and relieved 1st Bn Herts Regiment in Trenches B.3. Section. Casualty 1 other Rank wounded.	

WAR DIARY
or
INTELLIGENCE SUMMARY

Army Form C. 2118.

2nd Coldstream Guards

Hour, Date, Place	Summary of Events and Information	Remarks and references to Appendices
1915		
7th August	continued. On trenches B.3. Section. No casualties	
8th "	" " " " "	
9th "	Battalion relieved by 1st Irish Gds. Regiment had returned to Billets at the Queeng. In Billets at the Queeng.	
10th "	" " " " "	
11th "	Battalion paraded at dark and relieved 1st Irish Gds Regiment in the trenches B.3. Section. No casualty. In trenches, very quiet. No casualty.	
12th "	" " " " Casualty. 1 other rank wounded	

Army Form C. 2118.

WAR DIARY
or
INTELLIGENCE SUMMARY.
(Erase heading not required.)

2nd Bn Coldstream Guards

Hour, Date, Place	Summary of Events and Information	Remarks and references to Appendices
1915		
13th August	Continued. In Trenches B.3. Sector, a quiet day. Casualty 1 Other Rank wounded. Battalion relieved by 1st Bn Scots Regiment at dark and returned to Billet at Le Quesnoy.	
14th August	In Billet at Le Quesnoy. Casualty 1 Other Rank wounded whilst wiring troops in graves of officers and N.C.O and men at Windy Cemetery.	
15th August	In Billet at Le Quesnoy. Battalion paraded at 2.0 p.m. and marched to Vendin-lez-Bethune and went into Billet.	

WAR DIARY
or
INTELLIGENCE SUMMARY.

2nd Bn Coldstream Guards

Army Form C. 2118.

Hour, Date, Place	Summary of Events and Information	Remarks and references to Appendices
1916		
16th August	Continued.	
17th "	In Billets at Vendin-lez-Béthune	
18th "	— " —	
18th "	— " —	
19th "	Battalion paraded at 8.45 am and marched in Brigade via Chocques & Lillers, going into Billets at Molinghem (11 miles). During the march the G.O.C 2nd Division (Major Genl. H.S. Horne C.B.) watched the Brigade march past.	
20th "	The Battalion paraded at 8.40 am and marched in Brigade via Aire and Racquinghem going into Billets at Renescure (10 miles). During the march the G.O.C. 1st Army.	

WAR DIARY
or
INTELLIGENCE SUMMARY

(Erase heading not required.)

Army Form C. 2118.

2nd Bn. Coldstream Guards

Hour, Date, Place	Summary of Events and Information	Remarks and references to Appendices
1915		
20th August	Continued.	
	(General de B. Haig, 2.S.O, C.S.O. etc) watched the Brigade march past.	
21st	The Battalion turned out 6.30 am and marched via Brigade via Argues and St. Omer, going into Billet at Moulle (9 miles) Marching through St. Omer, the Brigade was inspected by the Commander in Chief (Field Marshal Sir John French K.C.B., O.M.) etc etc obtained scheme General Staff Officers tooled with the G.H.Q. Staff. Quarters Billet at Moulle.	
22nd	— " —	— " —
23rd	— " —	— " —

Army Form C. 2118.

WAR DIARY
or
INTELLIGENCE SUMMARY.
(Erase heading not required.)

2nd Bn Coldstream Guards

Hour, Date, Place	Summary of Events and Information	Remarks and references to Appendices
1915		
24th August	Enlonmer. The Battalion paraded at 8 am and marched via Cornette, Quilmes - Lumbres and Wavrans Ferry into Billet at Ouve-Wirquin. (13 miles) In accordance through Wavrans the Battalion joined the Brig of the newly formed 4th Gds Division Guards (Division).	
25th August	The Battalion paraded at 8.30 am and marched via (St Martin d'Harding Hem-Fauquembergues - Renty and went into Billet at Verchocq. (8 miles)	
26th August	In Billet at Verchocq	
27th "	" "	

Army Form C. 2118.

WAR DIARY
or
INTELLIGENCE SUMMARY.

2nd/9nd Alabama George

(Erase heading not required.)

Instructions regarding War Diaries and Intelligence Summaries are contained in F.S. Regs., Part II. and the Staff Manual respectively. Title pages will be prepared in manuscript.

Hour, Date, Place	Summary of Events and Information	Remarks and references to Appendices
1915		
27th August	Continued heat: had that having been attached to command the 23rd Infantry Brigade this day handed over command of the Battalion to Major P.A. Wagner D.S.O. On Duty at Pinchong	
28th "	— " —	
29th "	— " —	
30th "	— " —	
31st "	— " —	

J.S. Murdock Captain
for officer commanding
2nd/9nd Alabama George

1st September 1915.

1st Guards Brigade.
Guards Division.

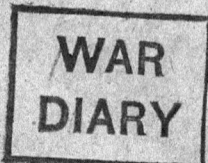

2nd BATTN. COLDSTREAM GUARDS.

S E P T E M B E R

1 9 1 5

On His Majesty's Service.

354

Army Form C. 2118.

WAR DIARY
or
INTELLIGENCE SUMMARY.
(Erase heading not required.) 2nd Bn "Coldstream" Guards.

Hour, Date, Place	Summary of Events and Information	Remarks and references to Appendices
1915		
1st September 1915	In Billet at Verchocq	
2nd "	" " "	
3rd "	" " "	
4th "	" " "	
5th "	" " "	
6th "	" " "	
7th "	" " "	
8th "	" " "	
9th "	Battalion at Assault en plein Digging	
10th "	" " "	
11th "	" " "	
12th "	" " "	
13th "	In Billet at Verchocq	
14th "	" " "	
15th "	" " "	
16th "	" " "	
17th "	" " "	
18th "	" " "	
19th "	" " "	
20th "	" " "	

Army Form C. 2118.

WAR DIARY
OF
INTELLIGENCE SUMMARY.
(Erase heading not required.)

2nd Bn Coldstream Guards

Instructions regarding War Diaries and Intelligence Summaries are contained in F.S. Regs., Part II. and the Staff Manual respectively. Title pages will be prepared in manuscript.

Hour, Date, Place	Summary of Events and Information	Remarks and references to Appendices
1915.		
21st September 1915.	In Billets at Verbocq.	
22nd "	Bn Marched to Dommiereneg & Billeted for night	
23rd "	Bn marched to Nesonchise, a very wet march went into Billet at that village.	
24 " "	In Billet at Nesonchise.	
25 " "	Bn marched to Auchel and went into Billet arriving about 9.30 am. Battalion paraded again at 1pm & marched to Noeux-les-Mines, arriving about 10pm & went into Billets. A very wet march, there were constant halts every few yards which caused the march to take twice as long as was necessary.	

Army Form C. 2118.

WAR DIARY
or
INTELLIGENCE SUMMARY.   2nd Bn Coldstream Guards

(Erase heading not required.)

Hour, Date, Place	Summary of Events and Information	Remarks and references to Appendices
26th September 1915.	Bn. paraded about 1 pm, marched via Sailly La Bourse, Vermelles & La Rutoire and went into Reserve in the Old British Front line about 5.30 pm. In going through Vermelles the Bn. encountered a good deal of Gas, he enemy shelling the Village with Gas Shells. Later in the evening orders were received to take over the New British line from the 21st Division. This was carried out & completed about 4 am on 27th.	
27th 28th	The Battalion spent these days in consolidating the New line, bringing up stores from the front, collecting range finders, arms & equipment.	
29th 30th	of the Bn. we has relieved. During these days the enemy shelled our New Trenches fairly consistently.	

Army Form C. 2118.

WAR DIARY
or
INTELLIGENCE SUMMARY.

(Erase heading not required.)

2nd Bn Coldstream Guards

Instructions regarding War Diaries and Intelligence Summaries are contained in F.S. Regs., Part II. and the Staff Manual respectively. Title pages will be prepared in manuscript.

Hour, Date, Place	Summary of Events and Information	Remarks and references to Appendices
27th September	Continued:-	
28th	Casualties 27th. Officers Nil. Other Ranks Wounded 18.	
29th	Casualties 28th. Officers Nil. Other Ranks Killed 1. Wounded 6.	
30th	Casualties 29th. Other Ranks Wounded 1.	
	Casualties 30th. Other Ranks Wounded 3.	
30th Continued	Bn relieved by 1/K Bn Middlesex Regt & got out of the trenches about midnight & marched to Mazingarbe and went into Billets early on morning of 1st October.	

Gui Feilding Major
Comdg.
2nd Bn Coldstream Gds.

1st Guards Brigade.
Guards Division.

WAR DIARY

2nd BATTN. COLDSTREAM GUARDS.

OCTOBER

1915

On His Majesty's Service.

Army Form C. 2118.

WAR DIARY
or
INTELLIGENCE SUMMARY.
(Erase heading not required.)

2nd Bn Coldstream Guards

Hour, Date, Place	Summary of Events and Information	Remarks and references to Appendices
1st October 1918	In Biuets at Mazingarbe.	
2nd "	"	
3rd "	"	
	Bn. paraded at Dusk & relieved 1st K.R.R. Regt in Trenches East of Vermelles. Capt G.J. Burnett D.S.O was unfortunately Killed whilst going round the Trenches we were taking over, earlier in the day.	
4th "	In Trenches East of Vermelles. Boswell's Left Keep L/177 Gibb's Supply wounded (remained at duty) O.Ranks 1 Killed 2 Wounded.	
5th "	In Trenches. Lieut C.H. Wilkinson Wounded. O.Ranks Wounded 7.	

//Army Form C. 2118.

WAR DIARY
or
INTELLIGENCE SUMMARY.

2nd Bn Coldstream Guards

(Erase heading not required.)

Hour, Date, Place	Summary of Events and Information	Remarks and references to Appendices
5th October 1915	Continued:— Bn relieved by 1/4 Bn Scots Guards at dusk & came into Support Trenches. During the day the Trenches were considerably shelled by the enemy.	
6th "	In Support Trenches	
7th "	Bn relieved 1st Bn Irish Guards at dusk in front line Trenches East of Vermelles. Major E.B.S. Follett M.C. and O'Rourke joined	
8th "	Bn just before proceeding to firing line In Trenches E of Vermelles. Heavy Bombardment of Trenches & surroundings on both sides. Casualties Lieut E.St.L. Bousolot (W) since died of wounds O'Rourke Killed 9. other ranks 29 other ranks S (SH) remainder with Regt	

WAR DIARY
or
INTELLIGENCE SUMMARY.

(Erase heading not required.)

2nd Bn. Coldstream Guards

Army Form C. 2118.

Hour, Date, Place	Summary of Events and Information	Remarks and references to Appendices
9th October 1915.	In Trenches (E.J Nemille) Heavy Bombardment of trenches all day. Relieved by 1st Bn Irish Gds it took upwards to Support trench. Casualties Lieut Duffield Wounded O'Rourke Killed 5. Wounded 8 remaining 1 man shy[?] wounded, remaining at Duty.	
10th	In Support Trenches Lieut Jarvis Lieut Ferguson Joined Bn at dusk from Base Casualties 1 O'Rourke Wounded.	
11th	In Support Trenches Casualties O'Rourke Wounded 1.	
12th	In Support Trenches Relieved by Royal Berks & Essex Regt & returned to Billets at Vermelles about 7-30pm. Casualties Killed OR 1. Wounded 3.	

Army Form C. 2118.

WAR DIARY
or
INTELLIGENCE SUMMARY.
(Erase heading not required.)

2nd Bn Coldstream Guards

Hour, Date, Place	Summary of Events and Information	Remarks and references to Appendices
1915. 15th October 1915.	In Billets at Verquin.	
12 h " "	" " "	
15 h " "	" " "	
16 h	Leaves at 3-30pm & march into Billets at Vermelles. Casualties Officers Wounded 1.	
	Billets at Vermelles. Casualties Officers Wounded 1.	
17th	In Billets at Vermelles. Leaves at 5/30pm & marches back to Sailly la Bourse. Relieved by 1/4th Gordons.	
18th	In Billets at Sailly la Bourse. Lieut A Briggs & Lieut W.G. Edmonstone joins Bn from Base	

Army Form C. 2118.

WAR DIARY
or
INTELLIGENCE SUMMARY.
(Erase heading not required.)

2nd Bn Connaught Rangers

Hour, Date, Place	Summary of Events and Information	Remarks and references to Appendices
19th October 1915	In Brucks at Sailly la Bourse. No 3 & 4 Coys paraded at 1 pm } for trenches 1 & 2 Coys " " 4 pm } for trenches	
20th	In Trenches (East of Vermelles) Casualties Captain S.G.J. Taylor Killed. O Ranks Killed 4. " " Wounded 8.	
21st	In Trenches (C.O.P.) Relieved by 1/4 Bn Gloucester Gds & went to Support Trenches at Vermelles. Casualties Nil.	
22nd	In Support Trenches Vermelles. O Ranks Killed 1	

Army Form C. 2118.

WAR DIARY
or
INTELLIGENCE SUMMARY.

(Erase heading not required.)

2nd Bn Coldstream Guards

Hour, Date, Place	Summary of Events and Information	Remarks and references to Appendices
1915 23rd October 1915	In Support Trenches. Relieved 1st Bn Irish Guards about 2/30 pm Casualties Nil	
24th	In Trenches (E of Vermelles) Casualties OR anks Wounded 3.	
25th	In Trenches (E of Vermelles) Casualties OR anks 3. Lieut. A. L. Bonsor joins Bn from Brig.	
26th	In Trenches (E of Vermelles) Relieved by 5th Royal Berks Regt about 4 pm Marched back independently by Companies to Sailly La Bourse for Tea. Continued	

Army Form C. 2118.

WAR DIARY
or
INTELLIGENCE SUMMARY.
(Erase heading not required.)

2nd Bn Coldstream Guards

Instructions regarding War Diaries and Intelligence Summaries are contained in F.S. Regs., Part II. and the Staff Manual respectively. Title pages will be prepared in manuscript.

Hour, Date, Place	Summary of Events and Information	Remarks and references to Appendices
1915		
26th October 1915	26th Continued. Alt 4pm after tea the Bn formed up & marched back to Billets at Hoogenacre arriving 10.30 pm. Casualties Killed O/Ranks 1. Wounded do 4.	
27th	In Billets at Hoogenacre	
28th		
	Bn paraded at 9.30 am Marching Orders & on back to join remainder of Division to be Reviewed by H.M. the King but owing to the Majesty meeting with an accident the Review was not held & the Bn returned to Billets about 2.30 pm.	
29th to 31st.	In Billets at Hodynene.	

Mr Trefusis Major,
Commanding
2nd Bn Coldstream Guards.

1st Guards Brigade.
Guards Division.

WAR DIARY

2nd BATTN. COLDSTREAM GUARDS.

NOVEMBER

1915

On His Majesty's Service.

Army Form C. 2118.

WAR DIARY
INTELLIGENCE SUMMARY.
(Erase heading not required.)

2nd Bn Coldstream Guards

Hour, Date, Place	Summary of Events and Information	Remarks and references to Appendices
November 1st to 10th	Billets at Hazignuel. On morning of 10th paraded at 8-30am and marched into Billets at Calonne. Very wet & roads dirty. Bn had Dinner on Roadside & afterwards continued the march arriving in Calonne about 3pm.	
11th to 14th	Billets at Calonne. At 2pm on the afternoon of the 14th the Bn paraded & marched to Billets at Merville arriving about 3pm.	
15th to 19th 20th	Billets at Merville. The Bn paraded at 1-30pm & marched to Billets at Vielle Chapelle arriving about 5pm.	

Army Form C. 2118.

WAR DIARY
INTELLIGENCE SUMMARY.
(Erase heading not required.)

2nd Bn Coldstream Guards

Instructions regarding War Diaries and Intelligence Summaries are contained in F. S. Regs., Part II. and the Staff Manual respectively. Title pages will be prepared in manuscript.

Hour, Date, Place	Summary of Events and Information	Remarks and references to Appendices
November 21st	The Bn relieved the 3rd Bn Coldstream Gds at dusk in the trenches just left of Neuve Chapelle. Trenches in a very bad state.	
22nd	Trenches.	
23rd	Relieved at dusk by 3rd Bn Coldstream Gds and returned to Billets at Vieille Chapelle. Casualties for period O'Ranks Killed 2 wounded 4.	
24th	The Bn paraded at 3-30pm & moved into fresh Billets on the Main La Bassee Road at Pont du Hem.	
25th	Relieved 3rd Bn Coldstream Gds in trenches position just left of the one the Bn held on the 21st & 22nd	
26th	Trenches	

Army Form C. 2118.

WAR DIARY
or
INTELLIGENCE SUMMARY.
(Erase heading not required.)

2nd Bn Coldstream Guards

Hour, Date, Place	Summary of Events and Information	Remarks and references to Appendices
27th November.	Bn relieved by 3rd Bn Coldstream Gds at and continued to Billets at Pont-du-Hem. Casualties for period Nil.	
28th	Billets at Pont-du-Hem.	
29th	Relieved 3rd Bn Coldstream Gds in the Trenches at dusk. The same position as on 28th.	
30th	— Trenches —	

P. Ramsay
Lieut Colonel,
Commdg.
2nd Bn Coldstream Guards.

13 DEC. 1915

1st Guards Brigade.
Guards Division.

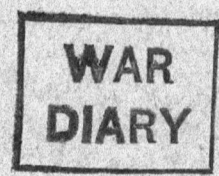

2nd BATTN. COLDSTREAM GUARDS.

D E C E M B E R

1 9 1 5

On His Majesty's Service.

Army Form C. 2118.

WAR DIARY
or
INTELLIGENCE SUMMARY
(Erase heading not required.)

2nd Bn Coldstream Guards

Instructions regarding War Diaries and Intelligence Summaries are contained in F. S. Regs., Part II. and the Staff Manual respectively. Title pages will be prepared in manuscript.

Hour, Date, Place 1915	Summary of Events and Information	Remarks and references to Appendices
1st December 1915.	The Bn was relieved in the trenches by 3rd Bn Coldstream Guards at dusk & returned to Billets at Pont du Hem. Casualties O.R. Killed 1.	
2nd	Paraded at 2pm & marched back to Billets at Merville arriving about 5pm	
3rd to 7th	Billets at Merville.	
8th	Bn paraded at 9am and went into Billets at Laventie arriving about 12-30pm.	
9th	Billets at Laventie. Company & Coy of 1st Bn R.W. Fusiliers attached for duty.	
10th	Bn paraded at dusk & relieved 3rd Bn Coldstream Gds in Trenches N.37 & P. Laventie.	

Army Form C. 2118.

WAR DIARY
or
INTELLIGENCE SUMMARY.
(Erase heading not required.)

2nd Bn Coldstream Guards

Hour, Date, Place	Summary of Events and Information	Remarks and references to Appendices
11th December 1915	Trenches North of Laventie.	
12th	Relieved by 3rd Bn Coldstream Gds at dusk & returned to Billets at Laventie.	
13th	Casualties for Prior 8 ranks Wounded 1. Billets at Laventie.	
14th	On relief 3rd Bn Coldstream Gds in Trenches at dusk North of Laventie. Trenches	
15th 16th	Relieved by 3rd Bn C. Gds at dusk & returned to Billets at Laventie. Casualties Nil	
17th 18th	Billets at Laventie.	
19th	Relieved 3rd Bn Coldstream Gds in Trenches at dusk. Trenches.	

WAR DIARY
or
INTELLIGENCE SUMMARY.
(Erase heading not required.)

2nd Bn. Coldstream Gds.

Army Form C. 2118.

Hour, Date, Place	Summary of Events and Information	Remarks and references to Appendices
20th December 15.	Bn relieved by 1st Bn Scots Guards (3rd Brigade) & returned to La Gorgue for Brigade Rest arriving about 5pm.	
21st to 24th	Bn rested at La Gorgue. On the 24th the Bn held their Xmas Dinner & everyone spent a very enjoyable time. The dinner was followed by a splendid Concert. La Gorgue	
25th & 26th	Bn paraded at 3pm & went into Trenches left of Rue Chapelle (Port au Herm) relieving 1st Bn Grenadier Gds (2nd Gds Bde).	
27th	Relieved by 3rd Coldstream in trenches and returned to Buvets at Port au Herm. Casualties Nil. Artillery very active on both sides.	

Army Form C. 2118.

WAR DIARY
or
INTELLIGENCE SUMMARY.

(Erase heading not required.)

2nd Bn Coldstream Gds

Instructions regarding War Diaries and Intelligence Summaries are contained in F.S. Regs., Part II. and the Staff Manual respectively. Title pages will be prepared in manuscript.

Hour, Date, Place	Summary of Events and Information	Remarks and references to Appendices
28th December 15	Billets at Port du Nieppe.	
29th	Relieved 3rd Bn in trenches left of Nulle Chapelle at dusk.	
30th	Trenches.	
31st	Relieved by 3rd Bn Coldstream Gds. returned to Billets at Port du Nieppe. Casualties 2 Privates } O'Rawe, 2 Wounded.	

P Whitfield
Lieut Colonel,
Comdg.
2nd Bn Coldstream Gds.

1st Guards Brigade.
Guards Division.

2nd BATTALION

COLDSTREAM GUARDS.

JANUARY 1 9 1 6

2/Oesterman 9.30

XIX
/
Sam
/
vol

Rds Div.

Army Form C. 2118.

WAR DIARY
INTELLIGENCE SUMMARY.
(Erase heading not required.) 2nd Bn Coldstream Guards

Instructions regarding War Diaries and Intelligence Summaries are contained in F.S. Regs., Part II. and the Staff Manual respectively. Title pages will be prepared in manuscript.

Hour, Date, Place	Summary of Events and Information	Remarks and references to Appendices
1st January 1916.	Billets at Pont du Hem.	
2nd do	Relieved 3rd Bn Coldstream Gds in trenches at dusk. Sector Right of Laventie.	
3rd do	Trenches. Casualties for period 3 O.R. Wounded.	
4th "	Relieved by 3rd Bn Coldstream Gds & returned to Reserve	
5th "	Billets at Pont du Hem.	
6th to 9th	The Bn paraded at 12.15 pm marched back to Billets. Went through Calonne arriving about 4 pm. Route:- Mair-Lohaves Rue La Gorgue:- Calonne. The Billets were in a very dirty state. Billets at Calonne. Brigadier General E.E. Seurin assumed command of the 1st Guards Bde from this day.	
10th & 11th	Billets at Calonne.	

Army Form C. 2118.

WAR DIARY
or
INTELLIGENCE SUMMARY.
(Erase heading not required.)   2nd Bn Coldstream Guards

Instructions regarding War Diaries and Intelligence
Summaries are contained in F.S. Regs., Part II.
and the Staff Manual respectively. Title pages
will be prepared in manuscript.

Hour, Date, Place	Summary of Events and Information	Remarks and references to Appendices
12th January 1916.	Bn. paraded at 11am marched to Buire N.W. of Merville arriving about 1-30pm. Billets very scattered but fair.	
13th to 15th	Billets N.W. of Merville. Pte Evans accidently wounded while at Bomb Practice.	
16th to 22nd	Billets N.W. of Merville.	
23rd	Bn. paraded at 8.45am marched to Rouge Buise at Pont-du-Hem arriving about 12 noon. Route Merville, La Gorgue, Pont du Hem.	
24th to	Bn. paraded (No Companies) relieved 10th Bn S.W.B in Trenches at dusk. Position Right of Laventie.	
26th	Stationary. Weather fine but Cold. Fairly quiet day. Casualties for Period 2 off. wounded. H2Lts (Winchilsea & Bruce) greatly improved since last tour of duty in same trenches. New Dug outs erected.	

(73989) W4141—463. 400,000. 9/14. H.&J.Ltd. Forms/C. 2118/10.

Army Form C. 2118.

WAR DIARY
or
INTELLIGENCE SUMMARY.
(Erase heading not required.) 2nd Bn Coldstream Guards

Instructions regarding War Diaries and Intelligence Summaries are contained in F. S. Regs., Part II. and the Staff Manual respectively. Title pages will be prepared in manuscript.

Hour, Date, Place	Summary of Events and Information	Remarks and references to Appendices
26th January 1916.	Bn relieved by 3rd Bn Coldstream Gds & returned to Reserve Billets at Port au Hern. Great precaution was taken during the night in case of an attack by the enemy in celebration of the Kaisers Birthday. Our Artillery was active during the night. Reserve Billets.	
27th.	Reserve Billets.	
28th.	Relieved 3rd Bn Coldstream Gds in Trenches at dusk. 2/Lt C.C. Heywood Slightly Wounded. 1. Oank Slightly Wounded.	
29th.	In Trenches. Quiet day. Cold but fine.	
30th.	Relieved by 3rd C. Gds & returned to Billets at Port au Hern. Casualties 1 Oank Killed 3 Oanks Wounded	
31st.	Reserve Billets at Port au Hern.	

P. Murray Lieut Colonel,
Comdg.
2nd Bn Coldstream Guards

1st Guards Brigade.
Guards Division.

2nd BATTALION

COLDSTREAM GUARDS.

FEBRUARY 1 9 1 6

2 Coldstream Gds.

Vol. XVII

WAR DIARY or INTELLIGENCE SUMMARY

Army Form C. 2118

2nd Bn Coldstream Gds.

Place	Date	Hour	Summary of Events and Information	Remarks and references to Appendices
Pont du Hem	1/2/16		The Bn. bivouced about 5pm & relieved 3rd Bn Coldstream Gds. in Trenches position left of Vielle Chapelle. Major Harrison (Instructor, Dublin University School of Instruction) attached.	
do	2d		Trenches. Weather Cold but fine. Water gone down considerably in Trenches Casualties for Period 3 O Ranks Wounded.	
do	3d		Bn relieved by 3rd Bn Coldstream Guards & returned to Bilets at Pont du Hem	
do	4th		Reserve Billets at Pont du Hem. Pvts Vivian & Penny joined Bn from Base & transferred to Machine Gun Company	

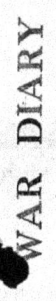

WAR DIARY or INTELLIGENCE SUMMARY

Army Form C. 2118

(Erase heading not required.)

Place	Date	Hour	Summary of Events and Information	Remarks and references to Appendices
Pont du Hem	23/3/16		2nd Bn Coldstream Gds	
			Bn relieved 3rd Bn Coldstream Gds in trenches at dusk. Weather cold but fine.	
	6th		Trenches. 1 O.R. Rank accidently wounded.	
	7th		Bn relieved by 1st Bn Coldstream Guards (2nd Bde) & returned to Billets at La Gorgue, arriving about 8 p.m. Lieut R.F.S Twining joined Bn from Base.	
	8th		Billets at La Gorgue.	
	9th		do. Lieut. Stewart Richardson & 2nd Lt Oakman joined Bn from Base.	
	10th		Billets at La Gorgue.	

Army Form C. 2118

WAR DIARY
or
INTELLIGENCE SUMMARY

(Erase heading not required.)

Place	Date	Hour	Summary of Events and Information	Remarks and references to Appendices
La Gorgue	11/3/16		2nd Bn Coldstream Guards. Billets at La Gorgue.	
	12th		The Bn paraded at 2-12 pm & marched to a point between La Gorgue & Merville, where they met the remainder of the Brigade and formed up to be inspected by Earl Kitchener. The weather was very bad pouring all the time, the inspection lasting only a few minutes after which the Bn returned to La Gorgue.	
	13th		La Gorgue	
	14th		Bn paraded at 10 am & marched through Merville to Billets at Caudescure arriving about 12-30 pm, weather fine but roads in very bad condition. Billets very much scattered & in a very dirty state on taking over from 9th Bn R.W. Fusiliers 58th Brigade.	

WAR DIARY
or
INTELLIGENCE SUMMARY

(Erase heading not required.)

Army Form C. 2118

2nd Bn Coldstream Gds

Place	Date	Hour	Summary of Events and Information	Remarks and references to Appendices
	15/3/16	—	Bn paraded & marched off at 8/15am to Buick at Gouverneskle. Route as follows:- Vieux Berquin, Strazelle, Fete. Weather fine but roads in bad condition. Bn arrived in Buick about 12-30pm.	
	16th		Bn paraded at 9am & marched to Buick in Huts about 2 miles W. from Poperinghe (Camp known as "C" Camp) The Bn arrived about 12-30pm after a very wet & windy journey.	
	17th to 24th		"C" Camp. During the stay of the Bn in Camp the weather was very bad raining or snowing every day & very cold	

Army Form C. 2118

WAR DIARY
or
INTELLIGENCE SUMMARY
(Erase heading not required.)

Place	Date	Hour	Summary of Events and Information	Remarks and references to Appendices
2nd Bn Coldstream Guards	15/3/16		The Bn paraded at 9.30am & marched to Cassel to entrain for Calais. Route as follows:- Road Junction L.2.a.3.7., Cross Roads K.16.B.8.8. Steenvoorde, Oxelaere to Cassel Station. The roads were in a very bad condition for marching it being very slippy. The transport had great difficulty in reaching the station. Dinners was served at the station & the train left for Calais about 5.30pm. Train journey very cold & slow arriving at Calais about 10pm. The Bn less 3 Platoons (which were left behind to off load the Transport) marched to camp about 4 Miles from Calais Station arriving about midnight. The Transport reached the Camp about 2.30am. The night was very cold & snowing all the time. The whole of the Battalion was under Canvas. Camp at Calais.	
	16/3/16 to 29/3/16			

P. Murray Lieut Colonel,
2nd Bn Coldstream Guards

1st Guards Brigade.
Guards Division.

2nd BATTALION

COLDSTREAM GUARDS:

MARCH 1916

7 Coldstream Gds.
Vol XVIII

Army Form C. 2118

WAR DIARY
INTELLIGENCE SUMMARY
(Erase heading not required.)

Instructions regarding War Diaries and Intelligence Summaries are contained in F.S. Regs., Part II. and the Staff Manual respectively. Title Pages will be prepared in manuscript.

Place	Date	Hour	Summary of Events and Information	Remarks and references to Appendices
	1916 March			
	1st.		Battalion in Camp at Calais.	
	2nd.		-do- -do-	
	3rd.		-do- -do-	
	4th.		-do- -do-	
	5th.		-do- -do- until 3 p.m. Battalion paraded at 3 p.m. and marched to Gare de Boulogne Station, Calais. Tea was had on arrival at the Station. The Train left about 5.30 p.m. and arrived at Cassel about 9 p.m. After the Transport had been off loaded the Battn. marched to Billets at Wormhoudt, a distance of about 9 miles. A most unpleasant journey owing to the Snow storm which lasted the whole of the journey.	
	6th.		Arrived in fairly comfortable billets, but very much scattered, about 12.30 a.m.	
	7th.		Billets at Wormhoudt.	
	8th.		-do-	
	9th.		-do-	
	10th.		-do-	
	11th.		-do- about 12 French and Belgium Officers accompanied by Major General G.P.T. Feilding D.S.O. and Staff visited the Battalion about 11.30 a.m. to watch the different ways in which the Battn. train when out of the Trenches.	
	12th.		Billets at Wormhoudt.	
	13th.		-do-	
	14th.		-do-	

1875 Wt. W593/886 1,000,000 4/15 J.B.C. & A. A.D.S.S./Forms/C. 2118.

Army Form C. 2118

WAR DIARY
or
INTELLIGENCE SUMMARY

(Erase heading not required.)

Instructions regarding War Diaries and Intelligence Summaries are contained in F. S. Regs., Part II. and the Staff Manual respectively. Title Pages will be prepared in manuscript.

Place	Date	Hour	Summary of Events and Information	Remarks and references to Appendices
	March			
	5th.		Battalion paraded at 7.15 a.m. and marched a distance of about 12 miles to "Camp" near Poperinghe arriving about 12 noon.	
	6th.		Three Companies were billeted in Huts and 1 Company in Tents.	
			Battalion paraded at 7.15 p.m. and marched thro' Poperinghe to "Camp D" arriving about 9 p.m.	
	7th.		Battalion in Huts at "Camp D"	
	8th.		Battalion paraded at 7 p.m. and marched to Railway Siding just outside Poperinghe where they entrained about 8.30 p.m. and after half an hour in the train the Battn. detrained at the "Asylum" Ypres and marched to Dug-outs on the Canal Bank on the left of Ypres.	
	9th.		Battalion in Dug-outs. Enemy artillery very active but no casualties.	
	20th.		Enemy commenced about 8 a.m. to shell the Canal Bank and continued until about 12 noon.	
			Casualties :- 2 Killed 8 Wounded.	
			Battalion paraded at 9 p.m. and relieved the 3rd Battalion Coldstream Guards in the trenches in front of St. Jean. Battn. Head Quarters were in the remains of Houses in St. Jean.	
	21st.		Battalion in Trenches	
			Casualties :- 5 Other Ranks Wounded.	
	22nd.		Battalion relieved by the 3rd Battalion Coldstream Guards and returned to Dug-outs on the Canal Bank. Relief completed about 11.30 p.m.	
			Casualties :- 3 Other Ranks Wounded	

WAR DIARY or INTELLIGENCE SUMMARY

Army Form C. 2118

(Erase heading not required.)

Place	Date	Hour	Summary of Events and Information	Remarks and references to Appendices
	March			
	23rd.		Battalion in Dug-outs on Canal Bank. Very dull day.	
	24th.		Snow fell during night 23/24th. weather very cold. Battalion relieved the 3rd Battalion Coldstream Guards in the Trenches parading about 9 p.m. The Canal Bank was heavily shelled during the relief.	
	25th.		Battalion heavily shelled during the day. 3/Lieut. W.A. Oakman Severely wounded. 3 Other Ranks wounded.	
	26th.		Battalion heavily shelled all day especially Battalion Head Quarters. Relieved by the 3rd Battalion Coldstream Guards at night and returned to the Canal Bank. Casualties :- 5 Other Ranks Killed. 7 Other Ranks Wounded.	
	27th.		Battalion in reserve Dug-outs. Report received "Mines successfully exploded at St. Eloi after which the 5th Corps occupied ground beyond craters, many German prisoners".	
	28th.		Artillery activity during the early hours. Battalion relieved the 3rd Battalion Coldstream Guards in the trenches in the evening.	
	29th.		Battalion in Trenches. Casualties :- Drill Sergt. A. Noyen Killed. 4 Other Ranks wounded.	
	30th.		Very heavy bombardment of our front line trenches and Battalion Head Quarters. Relieved by the 3rd Battalion Coldstream Guards	

WAR DIARY
INTELLIGENCE SUMMARY
(Erase heading not required.)

Army Form C. 2118

Place	Date	Hour	Summary of Events and Information	Remarks and references to Appendices
	March. 30th.		(continued) and returned to Reserve Dug-outs on Canal Bank. Casualties :- Lieut: A. J. W. Smith. Wounded. Lieut: W. S. C. Baynes. Wounded. 4 Other Ranks Killed. 23 Other Ranks Wounded.	
	31st.		Enemy commenced shelling Head Quarter Dug-outs about 7.30.a.m. when the Orderly Room and Officers Mess Kitchen were both blown in, killing Ptes. Jackson and Simpson. Casualties :- 2 Other Ranks Killed.	

[signature]

Lt:Colonel,
Commanding,
2nd Bn Coldstream Guards.

1st Guards Brigade.
Guards Division.

2nd BATTALION

COLDSTREAM GUARDS.

APRIL 1 9 1 6

2 Coldstream Gds

Vol XIX

WAR DIARY or INTELLIGENCE SUMMARY

Army Form C. 2118

(Erase heading not required.)

Instructions regarding War Diaries and Intelligence Summaries are contained in F.S. Regs., Part II. and the Staff Manual respectively. Title Pages will be prepared in manuscript.

Place	Date	Hour	Summary of Events and Information	Remarks and references to Appendices
Trenches	1.4.16		Battn. relieved the 3rd Battn. Coldstream Guards (under heavy shell fire) in the trenches. 6 O.R. wounded.	
	2.4.16		Relieved by the 1st Battn. Welsh Guards and retired to the Bull road near Asylum where they entrained and arrived at POPERINGHE about 2 a.m. and were billeted in very comfortable Billets. 10 O.R. wounded.	
Billets at Elverdinghe	3.4.16			
	4.4.16		Lieut. W.E.G. Bence, Lieut. N.N.Smith, Lieut. C.G. Rayward rejoined Battn. from Hospital.	
	5.4.16			
	6.4.16			
	7.4.16			
	8.4.16			
Billets at POPERINGHE	9.4.16			
	10.4.16		Battn. paraded at 6.20 p.m. and marched to Camp A arriving about 9 p.m. All the Battn. were billeted in Huts. Enemy fired many heavy shells into POPERINGHE and on the main road as the Battn. were marching out. No casualties.	
Huts at Camp A	11.4.16		2nd Lieut. J.R. Buckleberrys and G. Berkeley joined from England.	
Huts at Camp B	12.4.16		Major S.E. Vaughan arrived from England.	
Huts at Camp B	13.4.16			
	14.4.16		The Battn. entrained at 1.30 p.m. for YPRES and marched thence to POTIJZE and relieved the 3rd Bn. Coldstream Guards in the trenches. The 1st Bn. Irish Guards were on right & 4th Bn. Grenadier Gds. on the left. The relief was carried out quickly. No casualties.	
Trenches	15.4.16		Quiet day. Casualties 1 O.R. Killed. 1 O.R. Wounded.	
	16.4.16		Quiet day. Fire Hot. 1 O.R. wounded.	
	17.4.16		Quiet day.	
	18.4.16		Battn. relieved by the 3rd Bn. Coldm. Gds. and returned to Huts at Camp A. A very quiet and uneventful tour. Took Coy arriving in Camp about 2.30 a.m.	
Camp A	19.4.16			
	20.4.16		2nd Lieut. J.W. Burke joined Battn. from Base.	
Camp A	21.4.16			
Camp A	22.4.16		Battn. paraded at 6 p.m. and proceeded by train to YPRES. Relieving the 3rd Bn. Coldstream Guards in the trenches.	
	23.4.16		at POTIJZE. Relief carried out quickly & without casualties. 1st Bn. Irish Guards on right. 4th Bn. Grenadier Guards on the left.	
	24.4.16		Trenches. Enemy artillery very active on YPRES and St. JEAN. Casualties 2 O.R. Killed. 2 O.R. Wounded.	
	25.4.16		Very quiet day.	
	26.4.16		Trenches. Heavy bombardment on our right during the evening.	
	27.4.16		Trenches. Battn. relieved at night by the 1st Battn. Welsh Guards and returned by train to POPERINGHE. Last Company arrived in Billets about 1.30 a.m. Casualties 4 O.R. wounded (slight).	
	28.4.16		Billets at POPERINGHE.	
	29.4.16			
	30.4.16			

G. Vaughan Major
Commanding 1st
2nd Batt. Coldstream Guards.

1st Guards Brigade.
Guards Division.

2nd BATTALION

COLDSTREAM GUARDS.

M A Y   1 9 1 6

WAR DIARY or INTELLIGENCE SUMMARY

Army Form C. 2118

2 Coldstream Gds

Place	Date	Hour	Summary of Events and Information	Remarks and references to Appendices
1916 May.	1st		Billets at Poperinghe.	
	2nd		Do.	
	3rd		Do.	
	4th		Do.	
	5th		Do.	
	6th		Battn. Paraded at 6.30pm and marched to Huts at Camp "B" arriving about 7.30pm.	
			Huts at Camp "B". No. 2 Company found a Fatigue Party to erect barbed wire entanglements for trenches near St. Jean. The enemy were shelling the road heavily and the Company had the following casualties in the early hours of the 7th:- Captain A.W.E. Paley wounded. 13 Other Ranks wounded (6 Slight remained at Duty)	
	7th		Huts at Camp "B". No. 3 Company found a Fatigue Party for wiring near St. Jean. 1 O.R. Wounded.	
	8th		Huts at Camp "B". No. 1 Company found a Fatigue Party for wiring trenches near St. Jean. There were no Casualties.	
	9th		Battn. Paraded at 7.45pm and proceeded by train to YPRES, and relieved the 3rd Battn. Coldstream Guards in the trenches at POTIJZE. The Relief was carried out quickly and with no Casualties.	
	10th		Trenches. Quiet Day. Casualties 1 O.R. Wounded.	
	11th		Trenches. Very hot. Quiet Day. Casualties 4 O.R. Wounded.	
	12th		Trenches. Another quiet Day. Casualties 1 O.R. Wounded.	
	13th		Battn. relieved at night by the 1st Batt. Coldstream Guards, entrained at Asylum and returned to Camp "B". No. 1 Company remained behind to do a Wiring Fatigue. Casualties 6 O.R. Wounded. (2 Slight remained at Duty.)	

WAR DIARY
or
INTELLIGENCE SUMMARY

(Erase heading not required.)

Army Form C. 2118

Place	Date	Hour	Summary of Events and Information	Remarks and references to Appendices
1916 May.	14th		Huts at Camp "B".	
	15th		Huts at Camp "B".	
	16th		Batln. relieved the 3rd Batln. Coldstream Guards in the Trenches. Casualties 1 O.R. Killed. 10 O.R. Wounded. (3 Slight - remained at duty.)	
	17th		Heavy shelling during the afternoon. Casualties. Killed 2nd Lieut. N.L. Stewart-Richardson. Wounded 8 O.R. of which 3 were slight and remained at duty.	
	18th		A good deal of shelling in the afternoon.	
	19th		Batln. relieved by the 4th Batln. Somerset Light Infantry about 11 pm and entrained at Asylum YPRES at 12.30 am. Arrived at Camp M at 2.45 am.	
	20th		Batln. left Camp M at 3.30pm. and then marched to Billets at LONGUENESS. at 1.14 pm. arriving at ST. OMER at 3.30p.m. and entrained at HOUTOUTRE. Casualties to 19th. 5 O.R. killed. 10 O.R. Wounded.	
	21st		Billets at LONGUENESS.	
	22nd			
	23rd			
	24th			
	25th		Batln. left Billets at LONGUENESS and marched to Billets at QUELMES. Captain Gluttarbuck joined from Guards Division.	
	26th		Billets at QUELMES.	
	27th			
	28th			
	29th			
	30th			
	31st			

Chas John Trevor Colonel,
Commanding
2nd Batln. Coldstream Guards.

1st Guards Brigade.
Guards Division.

2nd BATTALION
q.

COLDSTREAM GUARDS

JUNE 1916

WAR DIARY
or
INTELLIGENCE SUMMARY.

Army Form C. 2118.

2 Coldstream Gds

Vol 21

Place	Date	Hour	Summary of Events and Information	Remarks and references to Appendices
1916 June	1st		Billets at Guelmer	
	2nd		" "	
	3rd		" "	} Battalion Sports
	4th		" "	
	5th		" "	
	6th		" "	
	7th		Batln. started at 7 am and marched to Billets at STAPLE arriving about 1 pm.	
	8th		Batln. paraded at 5.30 am and marched to Camp "L" near TOPERINGHE arriving about 11.30 am	
	9th		Camp "L". Batln. found working parties for burying Cables etc.	
	10th		Camp "L". " " " " " " " "	
	11th		Camp "L". Casualty - 1 Other Rank wounded	
	12th		Camp "L". " " " "	
	13th		" " " "	
	14th		" " " "	
	15th		Camp "L". 2nd Lieut. Laing Smith M.C. McWhirter joined Battalion. Batn. started at 8.30 pm and entrained near Poperinghe (L.5.c) and detrained at Meteren	

WAR DIARY or INTELLIGENCE SUMMARY

Army Form C. 2118.

Place	Date	Hour	Summary of Events and Information	Remarks and references to Appendices
1916 June	13th		YPRES about 10.15pm Batt took over Reserve Dugouts on Canal Bank. Casualties 1 Other Rank wounded	
	14th		Early heavy shelling during the day. Bath relieved the 4th Bath D.L.I at dusk & occupied old trenches. Casualties 2nd Lt P. Montgomery killed, 10 Other Ranks 2.O.R wounded	
	15th		Trenches fairly quiet all day. Enemy attack on the left at night. Casualties 2nd Lt E.M. Nixon wounded. Other Ranks 2 killed 12 wounded	
	16th		Trenches Heavy shelling during the evening. Casualties - O.R. 2 killed 4 wounded (Gas cases returned)	
	17th		Bath relieved about 10½ pm by the 3rd Bath Coldstream Guards and went into Reserve Dugouts Canal Bank. O.R killed 1 wounded 2. Removed at dusk/and/2nd Lt P. Butler Injury. Invalided to England	
	18th		Reserve Trench quiet day. Casualties - O.R wounded 6. (Remained at duty)	
	19th		Reserve Dugouts. Casualties O.R. wounded 2.	
	20th		Reserve Dugouts. Casualties Other Ranks wounded 4. (Remained at duty)	
	21st		Our artillery bombarded the enemy trenches during morning. Casualties 2.O.R wounded	
	22nd		Bath. relieved the 2nd Bath C.G. Commenced about 10pm. Casualties - 2nd Lt Butler Nurse gunshot etc.	
	23rd		Bath in trenches. Very quiet. Casualties - Other Ranks 1 killed 2 wounded	

WAR DIARY
or
INTELLIGENCE SUMMARY
(Erase heading not required.)

Army Form C. 2118.

Place	Date	Hour	Summary of Events and Information	Remarks and references to Appendices
1916 June	27th		Heavy bombardment by out artillery on German Trenches. Enemy retaliated in am and during the afternoon. Casualties Lieut R.H. Spencer Wounded & 2 Gunners of Batt.	
	28th		Enemy made a bombing attack on our grenadier post in the morning but with no damage to Batt. Scots bombarded the Fort commences about 10pm. The Relief was carried out quickly and Companies marched independently to our Huts at Camp "D" near POPERINGHE. Casualties 9 Other Ranks Wounded	
	29th		Huts at Camp "D"	
	30th		Huts at Camp "D"	

Jess Neale Lieut Colonel
Commanding
2nd Battalion Colegiean ??

1st Guards Brigade.
Guards Division.

2nd BATTALION

COLDSTREAM GUARDS.

JULY 1916

Army Form C. 2118.

WAR DIARY
or
INTELLIGENCE SUMMARY.
(Erase heading not required.)

1st 4th Bde

2nd Bn Coldstream Guards

Vol 22

Place	Date	Hour	Summary of Events and Information	Remarks and references to Appendices
1916				
July	1st		"Rutal Camp D."	
	2nd		"	
	3rd		"	
	4th		"	
	5th		"	
	6th		"	
	7th		Battalion paraded at 10.p.m. moved into Brigade Reserve. No 1, 2 & 3 Coys & 2 platoons of No 3 Coy were in dug outs on Canal Bank, remainder at the Chateau at Trois Tours.	
	8th		Battalion in Bripau Reserve	
	9th		"	
	10th		"	
	11th		" Casualties 2 O.R. Wounded	
	12th		Battalion paraded about 10 p.m. and relieved the 3rd Batt. Coldstream Guards in the trenches on the left of YPRES.	
	13th		Battalion in Trenches. Lieut. H.C. Kemberley joined Batth. from I.e. Casualties O.R. Wounded	

WAR DIARY
or
INTELLIGENCE SUMMARY

Army Form C. 2118.

Place	Date	Hour	Summary of Events and Information	Remarks and references to Appendices
1916				
July	14th		Trenches Casualties 2 O.R. Killed 4 O.R. Wounded	
	15th		Trenches Casualties 1 O.R. Killed 5 O.R. Wounded (1 Remaining at Duty)	
	16th		Battalion relieved by the 3rd Batln. Coldstream Guards and returned to billets at TROIS TOURS	
	17th		Brigade Reserve Casualties Lieut Col. G.P.S. Follett M.O. wounded 1 O.R. Wounded	
	18th		Reserve	
	19th		Battalion paraded about 10pm and relieved the 3rd Batln. Coldstream Guards in the trenches	
	20th		Trenches	
	21st		Trenches Casualties 1 O.R. Killed 1 O.R. Wounded	
	22nd		Trenches Battn. relieved by the 3rd Batln. Coldstream Guards and returned to their dug-outs Casualties Lt. H.E.E. Payne wounded 2 O.R. Killed + 6 O.R. Wounded	
	23rd		Reserve	
	24th		Reserve A/Lt Col. C.E. Hawkins DSO assumed command of the Battalion Major F.E. Vaughan to 3rd Battalion	
	25th		Battalion paraded about 10pm and relieved the 3rd Batln. Coldstream Guards in	

WAR DIARY
or
INTELLIGENCE SUMMARY
(Erase heading not required.)

Army Form C. 2118.

Place	Date	Hour	Summary of Events and Information	Remarks and references to Appendices
1916	July 25th		In trenches.	
	26th		Trenches Casualties 4 O.R. Wounded.	
	27th		Trenches 1 O.R. Killed. 4 O.R. Wounded. 2nd Lt. S. Sullivan and 2nd Lt. R.C. Fellowes joined Batt.	
	28th		Battalion relieved by the 10th Bn. Royal Irish Fusiliers and returned to Billets at POPERINGHE.	
	29th		Billets at POPERINGHE.	
	30th		Batt. proceeded at 9am. on march to PROVEN where they entrained to ST POL arriving about 5pm. From there they marched by road via to NEUVILLETTE reaching Billets about 8.30pm. Transport arrived about 12.30 am.	
	31st		Billets at NEUVILLETTE.	

W.S. Crawford
Lieut. Colonel
Commanding
2nd Bn. Coldstream Guards

1st Guards Brigade.
Guards Division.

2nd BATTALION

COLDSTREAM GUARDS.

AUGUST 1 9 1 6

2nd Bn Coldstream Guards

Vol 23

WAR DIARY
INTELLIGENCE SUMMARY
(Erase heading not required.)

Army Form C. 2118.

Place	Date	Hour	Summary of Events and Information	Remarks and references to Appendices
	1916. Aug 1st			
	2-10		Battalion paraded at 6 am and marched thro DOULLENS to SARTON arriving about 11 am. Billets at SARTON	
	11		Battalion paraded at 10 am and marched to BERTRANCOURT arriving about 1 pm. Billeted in huts.	
	12		BERTRANCOURT	
	13		— " —	
	14		Battalion paraded at 9 am and marched to billets at LOUVENCOURT.	
	15		— " —	
	16		Paraded at 11 am and relieved the 12th Bn Kings Liverpool Regt in the trenches opposite SERRE. Relief completed about 6 pm	
	17		trenches. 1st Bn Coldstream Gds on left. 1st Bn Irish Gds on right. Casualties 1 other rank wounded.	
	18		trenches. Casualties 10 rank killed 2 ORanks wounded	

40A

Army Form C. 2118.

WAR DIARY
INTELLIGENCE SUMMARY.
(Erase heading not required.)

Instructions regarding War Diaries and Intelligence Summaries are contained in F.S. Regs, Part II. and the Staff Manual respectively. Title pages will be prepared in manuscript.

Place	Date	Hour	Summary of Events and Information	Remarks and references to Appendices
	1916 Aug 19th		Casualties. Cavallies & E. Stubley wounded. 3 O.Rs wounded.	
	20th		Battalion relieved about 6.30pm by the 2nd North South Stafford Regt. Batton. concentrated at CORBIE for tea and then marched by Coys to Camp in	
	21st		BOIS de WARNIMONT	
	22nd		Camp	
	23rd		Battalion marched from Camp at 8 a.m. to billets at BEAUVAL arriving about 12 noon	
	24th		Battalion left BEAUVAL at 8 a.m. and marched to billets at MONTON-VILLERS arriving about 11 a.m.	
	25th		Marched at 10.30 a.m. to CANAPLES and there entrained about 2.40pm and proceeded via AMIENS to MERICOURT. Batton. then marched to billets at MEAULTE arriving	
	26th		about 11.15 p.m. Billets at MEAULTE.	

WAR DIARY
INTELLIGENCE SUMMARY.
(Erase heading not required.)

Army Form C. 2118.

Place	Date	Hour	Summary of Events and Information	Remarks and references to Appendices
Billets at MEAULTE	1916 Aug. 27			
"	28			
"	29			
"	30			
"	31			

Walterlinck Major
for Lt. Colonel,
Comdg. 2nd Coldstream Guards.

1st Guards Brigade.
Guards Division.

2nd BZATTALION

COLDSTREAM GUARDS.

SEPTEMBER 1 9 16

Army Form C. 2118.

WAR DIARY
or
INTELLIGENCE SUMMARY.
(Erase heading not required.)

2nd Bn. Coldstream Guards   Vol 2 ++

Place	Date	Hour	Summary of Events and Information	Remarks and references to Appendices
	1916 Sept 1st/9th		Battalion in billets at MEAULTE.	
	10th		Battn. marched to bivouacs and dug-outs at CARNOY.	
CARNOY.	11-13th			
	14th		At 8 pm the Battn. moved up to GINCHY and took over trenches from the 2nd Bn Grenadier Guards. Relief completed about midnight.	
	15th	6.30 am	At 6.30 am the Battn. advanced to the assault with 3rd Bn. Coldstream Guards on left and 1st Bn. Coldstream Guards (2nd Bde.) on right. Position of Companies:– No 3 Coy. left front. No 4 Coy right front. No 1 Coy left Support. No 2 Coy. right Support. On emerging from GINCHY WOOD the line came under very heavy machine gun and rifle fire and despite our Artillery Barrage, Casualties were very heavy. Two lines of trenches were captured and left and its original objective 1000 – 1200 yards away – was taken without great	

Place	Date	Hour	Summary of Events and Information	Remarks and references to Appendices
			opposition at 7.15 am. About 11 am the Unit again advanced and despite a heavy hostile Artillery barrage took the 2nd line. Lt. Edmonstone and Lt. Laing the only two officers left, went out 400-500 yards in front with men of No 1 Coy. and remained there till dusk when ordered to retire. Lt. Edmonstone was killed during the withdrawal. The Commanding officer and Lieut. Laing were the only two officers left with the remains of the Batln. Remainder of night spent in consolidating position. At 7pm a counter-attack by a few Germans on our right flank was easily repulsed.	
	Sept 16		After a fairly quiet night, the enemy shelled our position and lines in rear continuously throughout the day. Infantry on our flanks attacked the German lines with moderate success.	

WAR DIARY
or
INTELLIGENCE SUMMARY.

(Erase heading not required.)

Army Form C. 2118.

Place	Date	Hour	Summary of Events and Information	Remarks and references to Appendices
	1916. Sept.			
	17th		At dawn the Battn. after a quiet night, were relieved by the Lincolns and marched to BERNAFAY WOOD where they had a hot meal and then returned to their tents at the CITADEL. Battn. reaching in. Commanding Officer, Lt. L. Laing and 242 other Ranks approximate Casualties:- officers killed 4. Died of wounds 2. Wounded 10. Other Ranks killed (wounds) & missing 440.	
	18 & 19th		Quiet day in Camp. Draft of 200 men and 4 Officers arrived from 3rd (Guards) Entrenching Battn.	
	20th		Battn. marched at 7.15 p.m. and relieved the 6r. Bucks Light Infantry in the trenches opposite LES BOEUFS.	
	21st		"	
	22nd		"	
	23rd		"	

WAR DIARY or INTELLIGENCE SUMMARY

Army Form C. 2118.

Place	Date	Hour	Summary of Events and Information	Remarks and references to Appendices
Trenches	Sept. 24 & 25			
	26		Brigade attacked LES BOEUFS at 12.35 p.m. 2nd Bn. Grenadier Guards and 1st Bn. Irish Guards in assault. 2nd & 3rd Bns. Coldstream Guards in support. At 1 p.m. Battn. moved up and kept pushing forward behind assaulting waves, clearing trenches and LES BOEUFS village. Enemy put to flight. The night was spent in digging in the newly captured trenches about noon Capt. Verelst - Lt. Clarke & Lt. Macgregor killed by an explosion of Bomb Store caused by enemy shell. Second Line heavily shelled all day. Battn. relieved about 9.30 p.m. by 2nd Bn. Irish Guards and returned to bivouacs at CARNOY.	
	27		Battn. marched at 6.45 p.m. to camp at F.13 central (near MEAULTE.	

WAR DIARY
or
INTELLIGENCE SUMMARY.
(Erase heading not required.)

Army Form C. 2118.

Place	Date	Hour	Summary of Events and Information	Remarks and references to Appendices
	Sept 28"		Battn in Camp at F.13 central.	
	29"		Battn moved about 3 pm to a field camp a distance of about 1 mile.	
	30"		Battn paraded @ 2 pm and marched to billets at MORLANCOURT a distance of about 3½ miles	

M.H. Kirkpatrick
Major
Comdg. 2nd Battalion
Canadian Guards

1st Guards Brigade.
Guards Division.

2nd BATTALION

COLDSTREAM GUARDS.

OCTOBER 1 9 1 6

WAR DIARY

INTELLIGENCE SUMMARY

Vol 25

October 1916

2nd Bn Coldstream Gds
1st Bde

Place	Date	Hour	Summary of Events and Information	Remarks and references to Appendices
	1916 Oct 1		Battalion paraded at MORLANCOURT about 10.30 a.m. and marched about 2 miles where they entrussed and proceeded via CORBIE and AMIENS to HORNOY arriving about 7 p.m. and then marched to billets at DROMESNIL arriving about 7 p.m.	
	2 - 4		Billets at DROMESNIL	
	5	10 am	The 1st Guards Brigade paraded for inspection by the Major-General who presented medal Ribbons for Decorations recently awarded. Captain J.S. Coats, Lieut. H.R. Knosley and Lt. H. St. J. Thompson joined from 4 & Bn. Coldstream Guards	
	6		Billets at DROMESNIL	
	7		" " " Lieuts. L.H.L. Eccles, J.A. Anderson, H.C. Jacks and M. King joined from England	
	8 to 12		Billets at DROMESNIL	

Army Form C. 2118.

WAR DIARY
or
INTELLIGENCE SUMMARY.
(Erase heading not required.)

Place	Date	Hour	Summary of Events and Information	Remarks and references to Appendices
	Oct. 13		Billets at DROMESNIL. Lt. A.H. Kirk and Lt. G. Mann joined from England.	
	14 & 15		Billets at DROMESNIL	
	16		" " " 2/Lt. L.H. Cornish joined from England.	
	17 & 30		" " "	
	31		" " " Battalion paraded about 10 a.m. for a Rehearsal of the Divisional Review by H.R.H. the Duke of Connaught. K.G. &c.	

Mc Creafred
Lt Colonel
Comdg.
2nd Bn Coldstream Gds.

1st Guards Brigade.
Guards Division.

2nd BATTALION

COLDSTREAM GUARDS.

NOVEMBER 1916

Army Form C. 2118.

WAR DIARY
of
INTELLIGENCE SUMMARY.
(Erase heading not required.)

2nd Bn Coldstream Gds

Vol 26

Place	Date	Hour	Summary of Events and Information	Remarks and references to Appendices
	1916 Nov 1st		Billets at DROMESNIL	
	2nd		" " "	
	3rd		" " "	
	4th		" " "	
	5th		" " "	
	6th		Battalion paraded at 6.30 am and marched to the WINDMILL DROMESNIL where they embussed and proceeded via AMIENS and ALBERT to FRICOURT arriving about 5.30 pm. and then marched to Camp at MONTAUBAN arriving about 8pm.	
	7. 8. 9. 10. 11. 12. 13. 14. 15.		Camp at MONTAUBAN. Battalion paraded about 4 pm. and relieved the 3rd Battalion Coldstream Guards in the trenches near LES BOEUFS.	
	16.		Casualties:- Lieut. S.O. Cronin wounded (since died of wounds). Other Ranks:- Killed 2	

WAR DIARY
or
INTELLIGENCE SUMMARY.

Army Form C. 2118.

Place	Date	Hour	Summary of Events and Information	Remarks and references to Appendices
	16th		Wounded 10.	
	17th		Trenches Casualties: Lt. Col. E.B.S. Follett M.C. and Major H.G. Shaw Stewart M.C. wounded, other ranks wounded 5, of which 3 remained at duty.	
	18th		Trenches Casualties - other Ranks killed 1, wounded 5.	
	19th		Battalion relieved about 2 a.m. by the 1st Bn. Coldstream Guards and returned to MANSELL Camp. During this tour of duty the weather conditions were very bad - about 30 other Ranks being admitted to hospital with Frost Bite etc.	
	20th		MANSELL Camp	
	21st		Battalion paraded about 9 a.m. and marched to Billets at MEAULTE.	
	22nd		Billets at MEAULTE. Captain F.M. Gibbs rejoined	

WAR DIARY
INTELLIGENCE SUMMARY.

Army Form C. 2118.

Place	Date	Hour	Summary of Events and Information	Remarks and references to Appendices
	1916 Sept.			
	23	2:30ᵖᵐ	Battalion from Headquarters, 1ˢᵗ Guards Brigade and assumed command of the Battalion. Billets at MEAULTE.	

J.V. Gibbs
Captain
Commanding
2nd Bn Coldstream Gds.

1st Guards Brigade.
Guards Division.

2nd BATTALION

COLDSTREAM GUARDS.

DECEMBER 1 9 1 6

1st Guards Brigade.
Guards Division.

Army Form C. 2118.

WAR DIARY

INTELLIGENCE SUMMARY.

(Erase heading not required.)

2nd Bn. Coldstream Guards

September 1916

Place	Date	Hour	Summary of Events and Information	Remarks and references to Appendices
	1916 Sept 1st		Billets at MEAULTE.	
	2nd		" " "	
	3rd		Battalion paraded at 9 a.m. and marched into the COMBLES area via MARICOURT - BERNAFAY and GUILLEMONT. A halt was made between MARICOURT and BERNAFAY WOOD for dinner. Baton. arrived at COMBLES about 6 p.m. Companies being disposed of as follows:- Nos. 1 & 4 my Bn. LEUZE WOOD S/o 2t MALTZHORN FARM. Nos 3&4 Coys and Bn. H. Qrs COMBLES trench.	
	4th 5th 6th		COMBLES	
	6th		Battalion marched to SAILLY - SAILLISEL and relieved the 3rd Battn. 160th Regt. of the French 20th Corps 1st Battn. Irish Guards on Square U.8. MAP REF: 57.c.S.W.4.
	7th		in the trenches. 1st Battn. Irish Guards on the right.	
	8th		trenches. Casualties :- Wounded 1 other Rank. Battn. relieved by the 1st Bn. Coldstream Guards	

WAR DIARY
INTELLIGENCE SUMMARY

Army Form C. 2118.

Place	Date	Hour	Summary of Events and Information	Remarks and references to Appendices
	1916 Dec 8th		and marched to MALTZHORN Camp arriving about 12 midnight.	
	9"		Battn. paraded about 10.20 a.m. and proceeded by train from TRONES WOOD siding to the PLATEAU and from there marched to BRONFAY Camp.	
	10"		BRONFAY Camp	
	11"		Battn. paraded at 12 noon and marched to COMBLES area. Casualties: Other Ranks Killed 7, Wounded 9. Capt. H.E. ROSE, R.A.M.C. wounded (at duty)	
	12		Paraded at 5.20 p.m. and relieved the 3rd Battn. Coldstream Gds. in the trenches at SAILLY - SAILLISEL. Casualties: Lieut. E. Berkeley and Ensign. F.A. Corbitt wounded. Other Ranks Killed 1, Wounded 3.	
	13		Trenches. Casualties: Other Ranks Killed 1, Wounded 4, of which 2 remained at duty.	

WAR DIARY
INTELLIGENCE SUMMARY.
(Erase heading not required.)

Army Form C. 2118.

Place	Date	Hour	Summary of Events and Information	Remarks and references to Appendices
	1916 Dec. 14th		Battalion relieved by the 1st Bn. Coldstream Guards and returned to MALTZHORN Camp.	
	15th		Paraded at 10.30 a.m. and proceeded by train from TRONES WOOD siding to the PLATEAU and then marched to BRONFAY Camp.	
	16th		BRONFAY Camp.	
	17th		Paraded at 3.15 p.m. and from where entrained to TRONES PLATEAU and from where entrained to TRONES WOOD siding and then marched to COMBLES.	
	18th		Relieved the 3rd Battn. Coldstream Guards in the trenches at SAILLY-SAILLISEL. Casualties: other Ranks wounded 1.	
	19th		Trenches. Casualties: other Ranks wounded 1.	
	20th		Battn. relieved by the 1st Bn. Coldstream Guards and marched to TRONES WOOD siding and proceeded by train to the PLATEAU and then marched	

WAR DIARY or INTELLIGENCE SUMMARY

Army Form C. 2118.

Place	Date	Hour	Summary of Events and Information	Remarks and references to Appendices
	1916 Dec.			
	21st		to BRONTAY Camp arriving about 2 a.m. 21st. Casualties :- 1 other Rank died of Heart Failure.	
			BRONTAY Camp.	
	22nd		"	
	23rd		Battalion paraded at 12 noon and marched to the PLATEAU and from there trained to TRONES WOOD siding and then marched to COMBLES.	
	24th		Relieved the 3rd Bn. Coldstream Guards in the trenches. Casualties:- 7 other Ranks wounded 1.	
	25th		trenches. Casualties other Ranks wounded 1.	
	26th		Relieved by the 1st Bn. Coldstream Guards and entrained at TRONES WOOD siding for the PLATEAU and then marched to BRONTAY Camp.	
	27th		BRONTAY Camp.	
	28th		"	

WAR DIARY
— or —
INTELLIGENCE SUMMARY.
(Erase heading not required.)

Army Form C. 2118.

Place	Date	Hour	Summary of Events and Information	Remarks and references to Appendices
	1916 Sept. 29.		Battalion paraded at 5.15 p.m. and marched to the Plateau and from there trained to TRONES WOOD siding and then marched to COMBLES.	
	30.		Relieved the 3rd Bn. Coldstream Gds in the trenches.	
	31.		Trenches. Casualties O.R. wounded — 1.	

L.M. Gibbs.
Lt Colonel
Comdg. 2nd Bn. Coldstream Gds.

January 1917. Army Form C. 2118.

WAR DIARY
or
INTELLIGENCE SUMMARY. 2nd Bn. Coldstream Guards

(Erase heading not required.)

Vol 28

Place	Date	Hour	Summary of Events and Information	Remarks and references to Appendices
	1917 Jany 1st		Battalion relieved by the 1st Bn. Coldstream Gds. in the trenches at SAILLY-SAILLISEL and entrained at TRONES WOOD siding for the PLATEAU and then marched to BRONFAY CAMP.	
	2nd		BRONFAY Camp.	
	3rd		Battalion paraded at 10 am and marched via BRAY to billets at MEAULTE.	
	4th 5th 6th 7th 8th 9th 10th		Billets at MEAULTE.	
	11th to 23rd		Battalion paraded at 3pm and marched to Billets at VILLE arriving about 4.30pm. Capt. D. W. B. Hall joined Bn. from England. Billets at VILLE. During this period Company training was carried out also fatigue parties were found.	
	24th		Battalion paraded at 8.30 am and marched	

Army Form C. 2118.

WAR DIARY
or
INTELLIGENCE SUMMARY.
(Erase heading not required.)

Instructions regarding War Diaries and Intelligence Summaries are contained in F. S. Regs., Part II. and the Staff Manual respectively. Title pages will be prepared in manuscript.

Place	Date	Hour	Summary of Events and Information	Remarks and references to Appendices
	1917 January 24th		via MORLANCOURT and BRAY to BILLON Camp 16. arriving about 1 p.m.	
	25th to 31st		BILLON Camp 16. (Map reference A.25.? ALBERT 1/40000.)	

J.M. Gibbs
Lt. Colonel,
Commanding,
2nd Bn. Coldstream Guards.

February 1917 Army Form C. 2118.

2nd Bn. Coldstream Gds.

Vol 29

WAR DIARY
INTELLIGENCE SUMMARY.
(Erase heading not required.)

Instructions regarding War Diaries and Intelligence Summaries are contained in F. S. Regs., Part II. and the Staff Manual respectively. Title pages will be prepared in manuscript.

Place	Date	Hour	Summary of Events and Information	Remarks and references to Appendices
BILLON CAMP	1917 Feby 1st to 5th		16.	
"	6th		Battalion paraded at 8.30 a.m. and marched via MARICOURT - HARDICOURT - MAUREPAS to PRIEZ FARM (Map ref: B.6.a central ALBERT Map 1/20,000) arriving about 11 a.m. Baln. relieved the 1st Bn. Irish Guards in Reserve dug-outs.	
PRIEZ FARM	7. 8. 9.			
"	10.		Battalion paraded at 11 a.m. and marched to MAUREPAS RAVINE Camp arriving about 12.30 p.m.	
MAUREPAS	11. 12. 13.		"	
"	14.		Battalion paraded at 4.45 p.m. and relieved the 3rd Bn. Coldstream Guards in the	

WAR DIARY or INTELLIGENCE SUMMARY.

Army Form C. 2118.

(Erase heading not required.)

Instructions regarding War Diaries and Intelligence Summaries are contained in F. S. Regs., Part II. and the Staff Manual respectively. Title pages will be prepared in manuscript.

Place	Date	Hour	Summary of Events and Information	Remarks and references to Appendices
	July			
	14"		Trenches about U.19.d.2.8. (Map ref: ALBERT map 1/20,000).	
	15" to 17"		Trenches	
	18"		Battalion relieved by the 3rd Bn. Coldstream Guards about 7 pm. and returned to MAUREPAS RAVINE	
	19" to 21"		MAUREPAS	
	22"		Battalion paraded at 6.45 pm. and relieved the 3rd Batln: Coldstream Gds. in the trenches.	
	23" to 25"		Trenches	
	26		Batln. relieved by the 2nd Bn. Irish Gds. about 7 pm. and returned to MAUREPAS.	

Army Form C. 2118.

WAR DIARY

INTELLIGENCE SUMMARY

(Erase heading not required.)

Instructions regarding War Diaries and Intelligence Summaries are contained in F. S. Regs., Part II. and the Staff Manual respectively. Title pages will be prepared in manuscript.

Place	Date	Hour	Summary of Events and Information	Remarks and references to Appendices
	Feby 27th		Battalion paraded at 8.15 a.m. and marched via HARDICOURT - MERICOURT to the PRETERU thence by train to ANCRE junction, thence by march route to billets at YILLE.	
	28th		Billets at YILLE.	

S. J. Burton Major,
Commanding,
2nd Bn. Coldstream Gds.

Army Form C. 2118.

WAR DIARY
or
INTELLIGENCE SUMMARY.
(Erase heading not required.)

2nd Bn Coldstream Gds.

March 1917.

Vol "30"

Place	Date	Hour	Summary of Events and Information	Remarks and references to Appendices
	1917 March 1st		Billets at VILLE.	
	2nd		Battalion paraded at 10 am and marched via MORLANCOURT - BRAY to Camp 18. BRONFAY FARM arriving about 2 pm	
	3rd		BRONFAY FARM.	
	4th			
	5th			
	6th			
	7th			
	8th			
	9th			
	10th			
	11th		The Battalion paraded at 3.15 pm and marched via MARICOURT - HARDECOURT - MAUREPAS - COMBLES to FREGICOURT, relieving the 1st Bn Grenadier Guards in Brigade Support. Left Bedon arriving about 6 pm.	
	12th		The Battalion paraded about 6.30 pm and relieved the	

WAR DIARY or INTELLIGENCE SUMMARY

Army Form C. 2118.

Place	Date	Hour	Summary of Events and Information	Remarks and references to Appendices
	1917 March 12" (cont'd)		2nd Batt. Trenches in the trenches as Left Battalion of the Left Brigade. Casualties 2/Lieut V.B.L. O'Reilly wounded. O.R. Killed 7. Wounded 3.	
	13"		Inches trenches - killed 1 O.R. wounded 3 O.R.	
	14"		trenches. killed 2 O.R. wounded 7 O.R.	
	15"		Battalion advanced and occupied BRUNSWICK, GOTHA and COBURG trenches, which were unoccupied. Casualties killed 2 O.R. wounded 2 O.R.	
	16"		The Battalion was relieved by the 3rd Bedfordshire Regt. in the trenches about 7 p.m. and returned to pontoon support at PREGICOURT. Casualties Wounded 3 O.R.	
	17"		PREGICOURT	
	18"			
	19"			
	20"		The Battalion paraded at 5 p.m. and relieved the 3rd Bn Bedfordshire Guards in support of the outpost line	

WAR DIARY
or
INTELLIGENCE SUMMARY.

Army Form C. 2118.

Place	Date	Hour	Summary of Events and Information	Remarks and references to Appendices
	1917 Aug			
	21st		The Battalion relieved the 2nd Grenadier Guards on the outpost line of LE MESNIL – ETRICOURT.	
	22nd		The Battalion was relieved by the 1st Bn Grenadier Guards on the outpost line and returned to position in support.	
	23rd		The Battalion was relieved by the 6th Bn Kings Stafford Light Infantry and marched to camp in MAUREPAS RAVINE.	
	24th		MAUREPAS RAVINE. Divine service attended.	
	25"		"	
	26"		Fatigues	
	27"		"	
	28"		"	
	29"		"	
	30"		"	
	31st		"	

1. 9. 1917.

Eal Follett
Lt Colonel
Commanding
2nd Bn Coldstream Guards (?)

April 1917
2nd Bn. Coldstream Guards

Vol 31

WAR DIARY
or
INTELLIGENCE SUMMARY
(Erase heading not required.)

Army Form C. 2118.

Instructions regarding War Diaries and Intelligence Summaries are contained in F.S. Regs., Part II. and the Staff Manual respectively. Title pages will be prepared in manuscript.

Place	Date	Hour	Summary of Events and Information	Remarks and references to Appendices
	April 1917			
	1st		Camp in MAUREPAS RAVINE. Fatigues	
	2nd		-do- -do-	
	3rd		After the usual fatigues the Battalion marched via COMBLES and GUILLEMONT to camp at GINCHY arriving about 4 p.m.	
In the field	4th		Camp at GINCHY. Battalion working on MORVAL - ROCQUIGNY Railway	
	5th		-do- -do-	
			2/Lieut M. KING rewarded D.S.O., and L/Sgt W. FENTON awarded D.C.M for the capable handling of their men on March 15th when the Battalion advanced and occupied the enemy's trenches at SAILLISEL.	
	6th		Camp at GINCHY. Battalion working on MORVAL - ROCQUIGNY Railway.	
	7th		Battalion struck camp, paraded at 9 a.m, marched via MORVAL and encamped near LE TRANSLOY arriving about 12.30 p.m.	
	8th to 13th		Camp near LE TRANSLOY. Battalion working on MORVAL - ROCQUIGNY Railway.	
	14th		Battalion struck camp, paraded at 8.15 a.m. and marched via COMBLES - MAUREPAS - MARICOURT to Camp 13, BRONFAY FARM.	

Army Form C. 2118.

WAR DIARY
or
INTELLIGENCE SUMMARY.

(Erase heading not required.)

Place	Date	Hour	Summary of Events and Information	Remarks and references to Appendices
	April 1917			
	15th (Contd)		arriving about 1 p.m.	
	16th to 29th		Camp at BRONFAY FARM. Training	
	30th		Battalion paraded about 4 p.m. and marched via MARICOURT and HARDECOURT to MAUREPAS arriving about 6 p.m.	

1/5/1917.

G.J. Smith
Lt Colonel
Commanding
2nd Bn Bedfordshire Regiment.

WAR DIARY or INTELLIGENCE SUMMARY

Army Form C. 2118.

May 1917
2nd Bn. Coldstream Guards
Vol 3

Place	Date	Hour	Summary of Events and Information	Remarks and references to Appendices
	May 1917 1st		The Battalion paraded at 11 a.m. and marched via COMBLES – FREGICOURT – SAILLISEL and thence into ÉTRICOURT arriving about 3.30 p.m. and camped at ÉTRICOURT. The Battalion working on railway construction.	
	2nd to 19th			
	20th		The Battalion paraded at 9 a.m. and marched via CHERENCOURT – MOISLAINS – HAUT ALLAINES – CLERY & OURS and marched into MERICOURT. The Battalion paraded at 8.30 a.m. and marched via MERICOURT – BRONFAY FARM road – BRAY to MORLANCOURT arriving at 1 p.m.	
	21st		Billets at MORLANCOURT. Training.	
	23rd to 29th 30th		The Battalion paraded at 9 a.m. and entrained at HEILLY detraining at EDGEHILL (DERNANCOURT) and marched from the RENESCURE area.	
	31st		The Battalion detrained at CASSEL at 5.30 a.m. and marched to camp in the RENESCURE area arriving about 8.30 a.m.	

Rowell
Lt Col
Comdg. Coldstream Guards

WAR DIARY
or
INTELLIGENCE SUMMARY.

(Erase heading not required.)

June, 1917. Army Form C. 2118.

2nd Bn. Coldstream Guards.

Vol 33

Instructions regarding War Diaries and Intelligence Summaries are contained in F.S. Regs., Part II. and the Staff Manual respectively. Title pages will be prepared in manuscript.

Place	Date	Hour	Summary of Events and Information	Remarks and references to Appendices
	June 1917			
	1st to 9th		Camp at Anc ABBAYE DE WOESTINE, near RENESCURE.	
	10th		The Battalion paraded at 11.15 am and marched via ARQUES – LONGUENESS – TATINGHEM – ETREHEM – ZUDASQUES area arriving about 6 p.m.	
	11th		Billets in MORINGHEM – ZUDASQUES area, musketry practice on the TILQUES Ranges	
	12th		After musketry practice the battalion returned to camp at RENESCURE marching via ETREHEM – TATINGHEM – LONGUENESS – and ARQUES arriving about 7.30 pm	
	13th		Camp at Anc ABBAYE DE WOESTINE, near RENESCURE. Battalion Sports held.	
	14th to 15th		Camp near RENESCURE.	
	16th		The Battalion paraded at 7.20 am and marched via LES TROIS ROIS – ZUYTPEENE – WEMAERS – TILLIS in the OUDEZEELE – WINNEZELLE area arriving about 4 p.m.	
	17th		The Battalion paraded at 9am and marched via WATOU – PROVEN to camp in the PROVEN area arriving about 11 am.	The Battalion made the Rearguard in the Guards Division
	18th to 19th		Camp near PROVEN.	
	20th		The Battalion paraded at 7.30 am and marched to HERZEELE where they were reviewed by the General Officer Commanding 1st French Army, returning to Camp near PROVEN in the afternoon.	

WAR DIARY
or
INTELLIGENCE SUMMARY.

(Erase heading not required.)

Army Form C. 2118.

Place	Date	Hour	Summary of Events and Information	Remarks and references to Appendices
In the Field	June 1917			
	21st to 24th		Camp near PROVEN. Fatigues.	
	25th		The Battalion paraded at 9.45 a.m. and marched to camp in the woods in the area A.4.C. (Ref map Sheet 28) arriving about 12 noon.	
	26th to 28th		Camp in area A.4.C.	
	29th		The Battalion paraded at 8.30 p.m. and relieved the 2nd Bn. Irish Guards in the Support Line of the BOESINGHE Sector.	
	30th		Support Line, BOESINGHE Sector.	

Jas Black
Colonel
Commanding
2nd Bn Coldstream Guards.

Army Form C. 2118.

WAR DIARY
or
INTELLIGENCE SUMMARY.

(Erase heading not required.)

Instructions regarding War Diaries and Intelligence Summaries are contained in F. S. Regs., Part II. and the Staff Manual respectively. Title pages will be prepared in manuscript.

July 1917 2nd Bn. Coldstream Gds Vol 34

Place	Date	Hour	Summary of Events and Information	Remarks and references to Appendices
In the Field.	July 1st		In support in BOESINGHE Sector. No casualties.	
	2nd		—do— Casualties Killed 1 O.R. Wounded 3 O.R. 2 of whom remained at duty.	
	3rd		In support in BOESINGHE Sector. The Battalion was relieved at night by 1st. Battn. Irish Gds and platoons marched back independently to Reserve at ROUSSEL Farm, the majority arriving about midnight. Casualties Wounded 1 O.R.	
	4th		In reserve at ROUSSEL Barm. Lieut. G.P.FILDES to England. 2/Lieut. J.MOUBRAY joined Battalion.	
	5th		—do— Casualties Wounded 2.O.R. both remaining at duty.	
	6th		—do— At night the Battalion relieved the 2nd. Bn. Grenadier Guards in the front line, BOESINGHE Sector.	
	7th		In the Trenches. Battalion Headquarters, situated near BOESINGHE CHATEAU, were heavily shelled. Captain H.E.ROSE, R.A.M.C., Medical Officer, and 26842 Pte. J.W.BROWNBILL, R.A.M.C., were wounded by a shell as they were leaving the Regimental Aid Post, and both subsequently died of wounds a few hours later at No. 3 Field Ambulance. Other Casualties Killed 1 O.R.	
	8th		In the Trenches. A raid was carried out by Nos. 7 and 8 Platoons, No. 2 Company, an account of which is attached. (Appendix "A"). Casualties among the raiding party wounded 1 O.R. Other Casualties Killed 3 O.R. Wounded 6 O.R. Captain D.MC.VICKER R.A.M.C. joined Battn.	
	9th		In the Trenches. Casualties wounded 4 O.R.	
	10th		In the Trenches. Casualties Killed 1 O.R. Wounded 1 O.R. The Battalion was relieved by 1st. Bn. Irish Guards during the afternoon, platoons marching back independently to Reserve at CARDOEN Farm.	
	11th		In Reserve at CARDOEN Farm. Fatigues in the Forward Area.	

Army Form C. 2118.

WAR DIARY
or
INTELLIGENCE SUMMARY.

(Erase heading not required.)

Instructions regarding War Diaries and Intelligence Summaries are contained in F. S. Regs., Part II. and the Staff Manual respectively. Title pages will be prepared in manuscript.

Place	Date	Hour	Summary of Events and Information	Remarks and references to Appendices
In the Field	July 12th		In Reserve at CARDOEN Farm. Fatigues in the Forward Area. Casualties Wounded 6 O.R. one of whom remained at duty.	
	13th		In Reserve at CARDOEN Farm. Fatigues in the Forward Area. Casualties Wounded 3 O.R. one of whom remained at duty.	
	14th		In Reserve at CARDOEN Farm. Casualties Killed 2 O.R. Wounded 11 O.R. The Battalion paraded at 9.30 p.m. and marched to ONDANK Siding where they entrained. They detrained at PROVEN and marched to Camp in the PROVEN Area, arriving about midnight.	
	15th		The Battalion paraded at 11.30 a.m. and marched via HOUTKERQUE to HERZEELE arriving about 1.30 p.m. No. 9234 L/Cpl. A. SHILLITO awarded the MILITARY MEDAL for gallantry and coolness during the raid of the 8th. July.	
	16th		Billets in HERZEELE Area. Training.	
	17th		--do-- --do-- No. 13043 L/Cpl. F. GRAHAM awarded the MILITARY MEDAL for gallantry and coolness during the raid of the 8th. July.	
	18th		Billets in HERZEELE Area. Training.	
	19th		--do-- --do--	
	20th		--do-- --do--	
	21st		--do-- Major J.C. BRAND, M.C., left to command the 1st. Bn. Coldstream Guards.	
	22nd		Billets in HERZEELE Area. Training.	
	23rd		--do-- --do--	
	24th		--do-- --do--	

Army Form C. 2118.

WAR DIARY
OR
INTELLIGENCE SUMMARY.
(Erase heading not required.)

Instructions regarding War Diaries and Intelligence Summaries are contained in F. S. Regs., Part II. and the Staff Manual respectively. Title pages will be prepared in manuscript.

Place	Date	Hour	Summary of Events and Information	Remarks and references to Appendices
In the Field.	July 25th		Billets in HERZEELE Area. Training. 2/Lieut. T.H.PORRITT awarded the MILITARY CROSS for gallantry and good work during the raid of the 8th July. Lieut. W.G.OAKMAN and 59 O.R. joined the Battalion.	
	26th		Billets in HERZEELE Area. Training.	
	27th		--do-- --do--	
	28th		--do-- --do-- Lieut. A.I.STEEL and 15 O.R. joined the Battalion.	
	29th		The Battalion embussed about 8.30 p.m. in the Square, HERZEELE, and rode to the vicinity of INTERNATIONAL CORNER, where they debussed. They then marched to DE WIEPPE Camp, arriving about 11.30 p.m.	
	30th		The Battalion paraded at 10 p.m. and marched to the assembly position, about 2000 yards N. by W. of ELVERDINGHE.	
	31st		At dawn the Battalion advanced, crossed the YSER CANAL, passed through the 2nd. and 3rd. Guards Brigades, who had attacked and reached their objectives, and attacked and secured the crossings of the STEENBEEK. A detailed account of the operations from 31st. July to 2nd. August is attached as Appendix "B".	

Lieut-Colonel,
Commanding,
2nd. Battalion Coldstream Guards.

Appendix "A".

Account of a raid made by 2nd. Bn. Coldstream Guards over the YSER CANAL on the night of 8th/9th July 1917.

The Bombing Sections and Rifle Grenade Section of Nos. 7 and 8 Platoons, No. 2 Company, were organised into three groups.

The right group was led by No. 13043 L/Cpl. F.GRAHAM, the left group by 2/Lieut. T.H.PORRITT and the centre group, under No. 6210 L/Sgt. H.HARRIS, was detailed to hold the "mat head" at the point of crossing in the enemy's front line trench.

Lieut. W.B.ST.LEGER commanded the three groups from a place in the German front line opposite the mats.

Zero was at 10.45 p.m. At that moment the Germans put down an intense artillery barrage of 5.9's, 4.2's, and 77 mm. guns just behind our front line which lasted for sixteen minutes, and appeared to be as if the raid had been given away. But owing to the good leadership and great gallantry shown by the commanders the mats were laid across the canal and the whole party were in the German front line in twelve minutes and another three minutes elapsed before the Germans were aware of their presence.

2/Lieut. T.H.PORRITT'S party on the left worked their way along the German trench for 80 yards with bombs and rifle grenades killing two Germans and the remainder ran away. The right party went 60 yards and killed two Germans by rifle fire, obtaining the necessary identification.

The raid was to last fifteen minutes at which time Lieut. W.B.ST.LEGER fired three Green Very Lights which was the signal to withdraw. Both groups fell gradually back to the point of crossing and arrived there simultaneously and the whole party were back in our lines and the mats taken up in sixteen minutes, with only one man (No. 16712 L/Cpl. SIMKIN) wounded.

Appendix "B"

2nd Battalion Coldstream Guards.

Report on the operations of 31st July 1917 to 3rd August 1917.

Reference
Map :- ST.JULIEN. Sheet 28 N.W.2.
1/10,000.

At 5.30 a.m. the Battalion moved from its position of assembly at A.12.b., about 2000 yards W. by N. of ELVERDINGHE, in two parallel columns.

The right column consisted of No. 1 Coy. in front under Captain Viscount GAGE followed by No. 2 Coy. under Captain W.E.C.BAYNES, the left column was led by No. 3 Coy. under Lieut: A.W.KIRK followed by No. 4 Coy. under Lieut: B.V.BROCKLE-BANK; all Companies moving with intervals of 200 yards between platoons. The right column followed CLARGES STREET and the left column BRIDGE STREET.

After advancing 5500 yards the head of the Battalion reached the position of deployment, a lane running at right angles to the line of advance 1500 yards west of the Canal bank, at 5.20 a.m., and gained touch with the 2nd Bn. Grenadier Guards. From here the Battalion advanced in two waves, Nos. 1 & 3 Coys forming the first wave and Nos. 2 & 4 Coys. the second wave, with 100 yards distance between lines and 150 yards between waves.

There was very little hostile shell fire West of the Canal which was reached with only three casualties.

The enemy's barrage on the Canal was at times heavy but very consistent, which allowed Unit Commanders plenty of time as they approached it to see the gaps in the barrage to get through, and the whole Battalion got across the Canal without a casualty exactly to time, viz. 6.20 a.m.

On reaching the BLUE line which was the enemy's trench running parallel to and East of the PILKEM road in B.6.a. and C.1.a,

The hostile shell fire became heavier and casualties began to occur.

Here Captain Viscount GAGE and Drill Sergeant W.LAMB were wounded and several men.

Pressing on to the BLACK Line which was the road running N.W. to S.E. through U.25.c.d., the leading wave crossed at 7.45 a.m. according to time-table.

The hostile machine guns began to have effect and casualties increased, Lieut: R.C.G.G.LEVESON-GOWER was wounded and died soon afterwards.

The GREEN Line, which was the road running through U.26.b., was reached to time and the leading wave closed up to the barrage at 8.50 a.m. for the assault on the final objective.

-2-

~~began to lengthen their range.~~

The difficult manoeuvre of changing front half left in order to secure the GREEN DOTTED LINE was successfully accomplished, No. 3 Company pivoted on their left and swung their right round as No. 1 Company advanced. The objective was secured exactly to the scheduled time, viz:- 9.25 a.m.

No. 2 Company kept in touch with the 2nd. Battalion Grenadier Guards on their right. Touch with the left was difficult as the French right had been held up by a nest of Germans, but the situation was cleared up in the course of the day and touch was never lost again.

The two lines commenced to consolidate at 9.30 a.m. The Contact Aeroplane flew over the position and flares were lit. Unfortunately at this moment a German airman flew very low (about 100 feet) over the Battalion in a captured English plane with a black cross painted very indistinctly. The position of consolidation was therefore given away and a very accurate Artillery fire was shortly opened on the GREEN DOTTED LINE which caused many casualties. Lieut. B.V.BROCKLEBANK, Commanding No. 4 Company, was killed and Lieut. A.W.KIRK, Commanding No. 3 Company, was wounded, and 2/Lieut. L.G.LEGGATT of No. 3 Company was killed, leaving Lieut. G.R.M.CALDWELL the sole survivor. 2/Lieut. M.KING, D.S.O., was then sent up to assist Lieut. G.R.M.CALDWELL, who had taken over the command of No. 3 Company.

The sniping on the right began to increase as the day went on. 2/Lieut. T.H.PORRITT, M.C., of No. 2 Coy., was hit and died soon after, and all the Sergeants were killed or wounded, so No. 5208 Corporal W.KENT became Company Sergeant Major to No. 2 Company, which position he filled with the greatest skill. Shortly after this Lieut. W.B.St.LEGER was wounded.

No. 1 Copany meanwhile were digging in hard, but the ground was very wet and the ranks were getting thin, so they had no great volume of rifle fire as they were covering a front of 350 yards, and 2/Lieut. R.ATKINSON had been hit, leaving only 2/Lieut. L.W.G.ECCLES to assist Lieut. W.A.C.WILKINSON who was commanding No. 1 Coy.

At dusk patrols went out to reconnoitre SENTIER and PINSON Farms, and dispositions were made to advance further on their report.

At 10.30 p.m. the whole of Nos. 1 & 3 Coys. went forward 150 yards and occupied the Strong Point on their left front, SENTIER and PINSON, and consolidated under cover of darkness.

It now began to rain in torrents and went on all through the night and continued the whole of 1st and 2nd August. The trenches soon became mere ditches filled with water and the whole Battalion carried on under the most appalling conditions, everyone was standing in water up to the thighs and terribly cold.

Battalion H.Q. were in a concrete Block-house in an old German battery position, which was continuously shelled with all calibres without respite.

During the night 2/3rd August the Battalion was relieved by the 3rd Battalion Coldstream Guards and marched back over the Canal through ELVERDINGHE in mud up to the knees. So the first phase of the 3rd Battle of YPRES ended with the loss of 4 Officers dead and 4 wounded, and 175 O.R. killed, wounded and missing.

WAR DIARY
or
INTELLIGENCE SUMMARY.

(Erase heading not required.)

Army Form C. 2118.

2/Bn Coldstream [Guards]

Vol 35 August 1917

Place	Date	Hour	Summary of Events and Information	Remarks and references to Appendices
In the Field.	August 1917. 1st.		Trenches. Consolidation of ground gained the previous day.	
	2nd.		-do- At night the Battalion was relieved by the 3rd. Bn. Coldstream Guards, and marched to Camp near CANADA FARM.	
	3rd.		The Battalion was conveyed in Lorries to PLURENDEN CAMP, in the PROVEN area, arriving about noon.	
	4th.		PLURENDEN CAMP. Captain E.F.WALKER, R.A.M.C., joined the Battalion as Medical Officer, in the place of Captain D.MC.VICKER, R.A.M.C., who was wounded on 31st. July 1917.	
	5th.		PLURENDEN CAMP. Major E.P.BRASSEY joined the Battalion as Second in Command. Draft of 115 O.R. joined the Battalion.	
	6th.		PLURENDEN CAMP. Draft of 100 O.R. joined the Battalion.	
	7th.		PLURENDEN CAMP. Fatigues in the forward area. Casualties 4 O.R. wounded, two of whom remained at duty.	
	8th. to 10th.		PLURENDEN CAMP. Training and reorganisation.	
	11th.		PLURENDEN CAMP. Draft of 100 O.R. joined the Battalion.	
	12th.		PLURENDEN CAMP. 9967 L/Sgt. H.BADDELEY, 5208 Cpl. W.KENT, 8175 L/Sgt. A.H.LAMBERT, 14088 Pte. T.PUBLICOVER, 17558 Pte. W.MARSHALL and 9238 Pte. R.DEVLIN awarded the MILITARY MEDAL for gallantry and good work during the operations of 31st. July 1917. 2/Lieuts. F.H.G.HORTON-SMITH-HARTLEY and Hon. D.B.S.BUXTON joined the Battalion.	
	13th.		PLURENDEN CAMP. 7175 Sgt. J.E.CAFFREY and 8805 Pte. J.C.HEMMINGS awarded the MILITARY MEDAL for gallantry and good work during the operations of 31st. July 1917.	
	14th.		PLURENDEN CAMP.	

Army Form C. 2118.

WAR DIARY
or
INTELLIGENCE SUMMARY.
(Erase heading not required.)

Instructions regarding War Diaries and Intelligence Summaries are contained in F. S. Regs., Part II. and the Staff Manual respectively. Title pages will be prepared in manuscript.

Place	Date	Hour	Summary of Events and Information	Remarks and references to Appendices
In the Field.	August 1917.			
	15th.		PLURENDEN CAMP. 5200 Pte. F.GOODMAN awarded the MILITARY MEDAL for gallantry and good work during the operations of 31st. July 1917.	
	16th.		PLURENDEN CAMP. Draft of 138 O.R. joined the Battalion.	
	17th.		PLURENDEN CAMP. 18701 L/Cpl. H.NOLAN awarded the MILITARY MEDAL for gallantry and good work during the operations of 31st. July 1917.	
	18th.		PLURENDEN CAMP.	
	19th.		PLURENDEN CAMP. Captain W.E.C.BAYNES, Lieut. W.B.ST.LEGER, Lieut. W.A.C.WILKINSON, and 2/Lieut. G.W.P.FLETCHER awarded the MILITARY CROSS for gallantry and good work during the operations of 31st. July 1917. No. 6504 L/Sgt. F.A.SMITH awarded the DISTINGUISHED CONDUCT MEDAL for gallantry and good work during the operations of 31st. July 1917. Lieut. W.B.ST.LEGER, M.C., who was wounded on 31st. July 1917, rejoined the Battalion.	
	20th.		PLURENDEN CAMP. 2/Lieut. H.A.F.CREWDSON joined the Battalion.	
	21st.		PLURENDEN CAMP. The Battalion paraded at 4.15 p.m. and marched to PROVEN, where they entrained. They detrained at ELVERDINGHE and marched to Camp 200 yards West of BLEUET FARM, arriving about 7.30 p.m.	
	22nd.		Camp near BLEUET FARM. Fatigues in the forward area. Casualties Killed 2 O.R. wounded 2 O.R. 2/Lieut. J.A.ANDERSON awarded the MILITARY CROSS for gallantry and good work during the operations of 31st. July 1917. 2/Lieuts. E.F.LUTYENS and A.D.CROSS, with 92 O.R. joined the Battalion.	
	23rd.		Camp near BLEUET Farm. Fatigues in the forward area.	
	24th.		—do— After the fatigues the Battalion paraded at 7 p.m. and marched to ELVERDINGHE where they entrained. They detrained at BANDINGHEM and marched to PLURENDEN CAMP, arriving about 10 p.m. Lieut.Colonel G.B.S.FOLLETT, M.V.O., D.S.O., awarded the CROIX DE GUERRE by 1st. French Army.	

Army Form C. 2118.

WAR DIARY
or
INTELLIGENCE SUMMARY.

(Erase heading not required.)

Instructions regarding War Diaries and Intelligence Summaries are contained in F. S. Regs., Part II. and the Staff Manual respectively. Title pages will be prepared in manuscript.

Place	Date	Hour	Summary of Events and Information	Remarks and references to Appendices
In the Field.	August 1917. 25th.		PLUREMDEN CAMP. Draft of 8 O.R. joined the Battalion.	
	26th.		PLUREMDEN CAMP.	
	27th.		PLUREMDEN CAMP.	
	28th.		PLUREMDEN CAMP. The Battalion paraded at 1 p.m. and marched to PROVEN where they entrained. They detrained at ELVERDINGHE and marched to ETON CAMP, about 500 yards south west of BLEUET FARM, arriving about 4 p.m.	
	29th.		ETON CAMP.	
	30th.		ETON CAMP. A high velocity gun shelled the camp and vicinity during the day. 2/Lieut. A.D.CROSS and 92 O.R. who arrived on 22nd. were sent back to the 7th. (Guards) Entrenching Battalion. Casualties 1 O.R. wounded and remained at duty.	
	31st.		ETON CAMP. The Battalion paraded at 10 a.m. and marched to Camp near WOESTEN, just west of the main ELVERDINGHE-WOESTEN road.	

Lieut-Colonel,
Commanding,
2nd. Battalion Coldstream Guards.

WAR DIARY
or
INTELLIGENCE SUMMARY.

(Erase heading not required.)

Army Form C. 2113.

September 1917

Place	Date	Hour	Summary of Events and Information	Remarks and references to Appendices
In the Field	Sept 1st 1917		Camp near WOESTEN (ETON CAMP)	
	2nd		Camp near WOESTEN (ETON CAMP). (Camp shelled intermittently - no casualties).	
	3rd		Camp near WOESTEN (ETON CAMP).	
	4th		Battalion paraded at 6.30 p.m., and marched to trenches via ELVERDINGHE - BOESINGHE - WIJDENDRIFT relieving the 1st Bn.Welsh Guards in the left sector of the Brigade Area. (Lieut.W.G.Oakman and 3 O.Rs.wounded).	
	5th		Trenches near LANGEMARCK. (2/Lieut.H.A.F.Crewdson wounded - O.Rs. 3 killed, 3 wounded).	
	6th		Trenches near LANGEMARCK. (O.Rs. 2 wounded).	
	7th		Trenches near LANGEMARCK. (O.Rs. 1 killed, 3 wounded).	
	8th		Battalion was relieved by the 3rd Bn.Coldstream Guards, and marched to Camp EMILE FARM near ELVERDINGHE. (2/Lieut.R.V.Martyn wounded - O.Rs.,3 killed, 3 wounded).	
	9th		Camp near ELVERDINGHE (EMILE FARM).	
	10th		Camp near ELVERDINGHE (EMILE FARM).	
	11th		Camp near ELVERDINGHE (EMILE FARM). Camp was bombed by enemy aircraft. (O.Rs.3 wounded - 2 remained at duty).	
	12th		Battalion paraded at 3 p.m., and marched via MARGUERITE FARM - ZOMMERBLOOM - DE WIPPE cross roads to DUBLIN CAMP arriving about 4.30 p.m.	
	13th		DUBLIN CAMP. (Training).	
	14th		DUBLIN CAMP. (Training).	

WAR DIARY or INTELLIGENCE SUMMARY.

Army Form C. 2118.

(Erase heading not required.)

Place	Date	Hour	Summary of Events and Information	Remarks and references to Appendices
In the Field	Sept. 15th 1917.		DUBLIN CAMP. (Training).	
	16th		DUBLIN CAMP. (Training).	
	17th		DUBLIN CAMP. (Training). (2/Lieut.F.R.Poole joined).	
	18th		DUBLIN CAMP. (Training).	
	19th		DUBLIN CAMP. (Training).	
	20th		Battalion paraded at 7.50 a.m., and marched to PLURENDEN CAMP arriving about 12 noon. (Draft of 28 O.Rs. joined Battalion).	
	21st		PLURENDEN CAMP. (Training).	
	22nd		Battalion paraded at 1.45 p.m., and marched to PROVEN thence entraining to ELVERDINGHE, and marching to CAMBRIDGE CAMP 200 yards west of BLUET FARM. (2/Lieut.A.J.O.A.Bugler and 6 O.Rs. joined).	
	23rd		CAMBRIDGE CAMP. (Fatigues).	
	24th		CAMBRIDGE CAMP. (Fatigues). {Capt.W.E.C.Baynes,M.C.wounded - O.Rs.11 killed,11wounded of which 3 remained at duty). (Lieut.G.C.Firbank,wounded-remained at duty)}	
	25th		Battalion paraded at 5.15 p.m., and marched to ELVERDINGHE thence entraining to BANDAGHEM and marching to PLURENDEN CAMP arriving about 7 p.m. (2 O.Rs.joined).	
	26th		PLURENDEN CAMP (Training).(Lieut.R.C.B.Fellowes & 23 O.Rs.joined).	
	27th		PLURENDEN CAMP (Training).(Draft of 4 O.Rs.joined).	
	28th		PLURENDEN CAMP (Training).	

Army Form C. 2118.

WAR DIARY
or
INTELLIGENCE SUMMARY.
(Erase heading not required.)

Instructions regarding War Diaries and Intelligence Summaries are contained in F. S. Regs., Part II. and the Staff Manual respectively. Title pages will be prepared in manuscript.

Place	Date	Hour	Summary of Events and Information	Remarks and references to Appendices
In the Field.	Sept. 29th 1917. 30th		PLURENDEN CAMP. (Training). (2/Lieut.T.T.Barnard and 11 O.Rs. joined). PLURENDEN CAMP. (Training).	

October 1st, 1917.

Jn B hit
Lieut.-Colonel,
Commanding,
2nd Battalion Coldstream Guards.

Army Form C. 2118.

WAR DIARY
or INTELLIGENCE SUMMARY.

(Erase heading not required.)

Oct 1917 2nd Coldstream Gds. Vol 37

Place	Date	Hour	Summary of Events and Information	Remarks and references to Appendices
In the Field.	Oct. 1917. 1st		PLURENDEN CAMP (Training). 2nd Lieut. S.W.Lindres joined.	
	2nd		PLURENDEN CAMP (Training).	
	3rd		PLURENDEN CAMP (Training).	
	4th		PLURENDEN CAMP (Training). 5 Other Ranks joined.	
	5th		PLURENDEN CAMP (Training).	
	6th		PLURENDEN CAMP (Training).	
	7th		PLURENDEN CAMP. The Battalion paraded at 8.15 a.m. and marched to BANDAGHEM, entraining at 9 a.m. for ELVERDINGHE, from thence marching to Camp (CHARTERHOUSE) at B.9.8.8.2. - Sheet 28 NW 1/20000 - arriving about 10.30 a.m. At night Nos.1. & 3. Companies paraded at 5.30 p.m., and marched to trenches near KOEKUIT.	
	8th		Battalion Headquarters, with Nos.4. & 2. Companies, paraded at 5 p.m. and marched via BOESINGHE to trenches near KOEKUIT. Casualty: Lieut.A.I.STEEL Killed.	
	9th		At dawn the Battalion attacked and captured the first and second objectives. Detailed statement attached.	
	10th		Trenches.	
	11th		Trenches. At night the Battalion was relieved, and marched back to BENNETT CAMP.	
	12th		BENNETT CAMP.	

WAR DIARY or INTELLIGENCE SUMMARY.

Army Form C. 2118.

Place	Date	Hour	Summary of Events and Information	Remarks and references to Appendices
In the Field	Oct 1917. 13th		BENNET CAMP. The Battalion paraded at 9.15 a.m. and marched to ONDANK SIDING, thence entraining for LUNAVILLE FARM, and marching to BOESINGHE, arriving before 1 p.m. The Battalion bivouacked in BOESINGHE until 3.30 p.m., and then marched to trenches near HOUTHOULST FOREST. (Casualties: Other Ranks 2 killed, and 6 wounded, 2 of whom remained at duty)	
	14th		Trenches. (Casualties: 1 Other Rank wounded).	
	15th		Trenches. (Casualties: 6 Other Ranks wounded).	
	16th		Trenches. (Casualties: 1 Other Rank wounded). At night the Battalion was relieved, and marched to BOESINGHE. At 3 a.m. the Battalion entrained for BANDAGHEM, and then marched to PORBHESTER CAMP, arriving about 5.30 a.m.	
	17th		PORCHESTER CAMP. Lieut.C.G.HEYWOOD, 2nd Lieut.C.G.C.BALFOUR, and draft of 11 Other Ranks joined the Battalion.	
	18th		PORCHESTER CAMP. 2nd Lieut.A.H.G.BUTCHER, and 50 Other Ranks joined the Battalion.	
	19th		PORCHESTER CAMP. The Battalion paraded at 5.45 a.m., and marched to PROVEN, entraining at 6.15 a.m. for WATTEN. On arrival at WATTEN the Battalion marched to billets at LA COMMUNE. Draft of 87 Other Ranks joined.	
	20th		Billets at LA COMMUNE. Draft of 4 Other Ranks joined.	
	21st		Billets at LA COMMUNE.	
	22nd		Billets at LA COMMUNE.	
	23rd		Billets at LA COMMUNE.	
	24th		Billets at LA COMMUNE. Lieut.E.J.WATSON SMITH, 2nd Lieut.H.W.LAKE, and 2 Other Ranks joined.	

Army Form C. 2118.

WAR DIARY
or
INTELLIGENCE SUMMARY.

(Erase heading not required.)

Place	Date	Hour	Summary of Events and Information	Remarks and references to Appendices
In the Field.	October 1917. 25th		Billets at LA COMMUNE. The Guards Division was reviewed by the Commander-in-Chief near CULEM. Draft of 4 Other Ranks joined).	
	26th		Billets at LA COMMUNE. (Training).	
	27th		Billets at LA COMMUNE. (Training).	
	28th		Billets at LA COMMUNE. (Training). Draft of 3 Other Ranks joined.	
	29th		Billets at LA COMMUNE. (Training). Lieut.G.BARRY and draft of 99 Other Ranks joined, also draft of 18 O.Rs.(Signallers)	
	30th		Billets at LA COMMUNE. (Training).	
	31st		Billets at LA COMMUNE. (Training). The undermentioned N.C.O's. and Men of the Battalion were awarded the MILITARY MEDAL for gallantry and good work during the operations of the 9th October. 9392. Sgt. W.FLEMING. 8853. Sgt. E.GRAINGER. 12724. L/C. J.VARTY. 18419. L/C. A.BESWICK. 13264. L/C. R.FORSTER. 15236. " F.J.PECK. 9528. " J.SIMPSON. 14401. L/C. G.W.RONSON. 17508. Pte. W.E.PATEMAN. 8788. Pte. A.CLAYTON. 16152. Pte. J.WETHERTON. 16090. " T.STREET. 16022. " R.J.BROOKS. 10853. " A.CHESHIRE. 18970. " W.CLARKE. 18309. " A.V.BURNS. 9991. " M.CHARLTON. 9745. " T.PORTON. 10462. " L.HOWARTH. 9671. " A.WALE. 10984. " A.E.BUTLER. (attd. 8691. " F.H.BOYER.,R.A.M.C. 1st Gds.Bde.T.M.Batty.)	

November 1st, 1917.

[signature]
Lieut.-Colonel,
Commanding,
2nd Battalion Coldstream Guards.

R E P O R T on the advance
over the BROEMBEEK. Oct. 9th - 10th.

Reference Map:- BROEMBEEK.

By midnight in the night of October 8th/9th, the Battalion was in position in the assembly area in PANTHER TRENCH from U.16.d.85.20. - U.16. c.87.22. with Battalion Headquarters at CANNES FARM. The Battalion was commanded by Major E.P.BRASSEY with Lieut.C.J.R.SYMONS as Adjutant, Capt. H.J.R.BRIERLY in reserve, and Capt. J.WALKER R.A.M.C. attached.

No.1.Company was commanded by Capt.H.O.St.J.THOMPSON with Lieut. G.C.FIRBANK, and 2nd Lieut.L.W.G.ECCLES.

No.2.Company was commanded by Capt.The Hon.H.S.FEILDING, with 2nd Lieut.J.MOUBRAY and 2nd Lieut.The Hon.D.B.S.BUXTON.

No.3.Company was commanded by Lieut.A.I.STEEL with Lieut.P.H.G. HOXTON-SMITHERLETLEY, and 2nd Lieut.R.C.J.DRUMMOND.

No.4.Company was commanded by Lieut.W.G.OAKMAN with 2nd Lieut. F.H.LUTHIS and 2nd Lieut.F.H.MARTIN.

During the evening of the 8th, rain fell incessingly, and the ground gradually became a morass, but preparations had to be carried on with, and parties were despatched to get up rations, to distribute mats along the front for crossing the BROEMBEEK, and to cut the wire in front.

This was not completed until 2 a.m., and the majority of the men were much exhausted, wet through and chilled to the bone, and five men who had sunk in the mud over the waist and had to be dug out were put out of action from exhaustion. The heavy rains were making the BROEMBEEK rise continuously, and anxious moments were endured during the next three hours before zero as to whether the men would not be too exhausted to attack when the moment came to start.

No.1.Company on the right, and No.3.Company on the left were in front, as they formed the first two waves to take the first objective, which was across the main KOEKUIT ROAD in a line U.16.B.0.9. to U.17.a.7.8. No.2.Company on the right, and No.4.Company on the left found the third and fourth waves, and went through Nos.1. & 3. Companies, after the first objective had been taken, to take the second objective in a line U.11.b.1.1. U.11.d.9.9.known as OXFORD BLDG. Each Company had one Platoon as Moppers up. The distance to the first objective was 950 yards, and to the 2nd 1800 yards.

- 1 -

Sheet No.2.

The 2nd Bn. Grenadier Guards were on the right, and the 1st Bn. Scots Guards (2nd Guards Brigade) on the left.

At 5.20 a.m. the signal to start was given by an intense barrage of guns on the BROEMBEEK, and of Stokes Mortars beyond the stream.

All four Companies went forward in formation, but well closed up to avoid the expected German barrage on PANTHER TRENCH, and got down to the edge of the stream in good time, but it was found to be impossible to carry the mats owing to the state of the ground, and so they were thrown away, some men crossed the stream on bridges and fallen trees, but the majority plunged in up to the waist and waded across. It was just at this moment that all the Germans holding their advanced posts rushed out to surrender, and went back through our lines, reaching Battalion Headquarters ten minutes after the commencement of the attack.

This put great heart into the men, and forgetting all the miseries of the previous night, pushed forward in perfect lines, having reformed under the far bank of the BROEMBEEK. It was found that the Germans opposite the Battalion were the 6th Bavarian Infantry Regiment of the 6th Bavarian Division. They had just come into the line having completed the relief at 4 a.m., an hour and twenty minutes before the attack commenced, so they knew nothing about their front, and were completely surprised by our assault.

After crossing the BROEMBEEK, the ground was much better going and drier. Nos.1. & 3. Companies reached their objective to time, viz: 5.12 a.m. without much difficulty as there were no serious obstacles in the shape of concrete blockhouses to overcome.

The barrage rested four minutes on the BROEMBEEK, and then lifting one hundred yards remaining for six minutes, after that it moved slowly forward at the rate of 100 yards in six minutes, and rested 45 minutes on the first objective. From the first objective, it moved at 100 yards in eight minutes and rested on the second objective for 45 minutes. So the pace was very slow, and Companies had plenty of time to reform after crossing the stream, and if anything went wrong there was plenty of time to catch up the barrage again. Casualties began to occur from the first movement.

Lieut. A.I. STEEL had been killed during the night 7th/8th, and

Sheet No.3.

Lieut. P.H.G. HORTON-SMITH-HARTLEY had assumed command of No.3. Company.

Capt. The Hon. H.S. FEILDING was badly wounded, and died two hours after, before reaching the BROEMBEEK, and 2nd Lieut. L.W.G. ECCLES was wounded soon after crossing the stream, and several men had fallen.

In advancing on the 1st objective, it was found that the barrage had successfully dealt with the enemys so called "Shell-Hole method" of defence, and the occupants had mostly been killed or wounded. A good many surrendered, and the remainder were running away. This was the cause of a good many casualties, as the front Companies full of ardour pressed on after them, and in some cases actually running, and got into our own barrage.

Just before reaching the first objective, 2nd Lieut. F.H. LUTYENS was wounded as well as 2nd Lieut. J. MOUBRAY which now left 2nd Lieut. The Hon. D.B.S. BUXTON alone with No.2. Company.

At 7 a.m. Nos.2. & 4. Companies deployed their leading line, and closing up to the barrage passed through Nos.1. & 3. Companies, who were now digging in, and commenced to advance on the second objective. No.4. Company had not much opposition, but No.2. Company were confronted with a collection of blockhouses known as VEE BEND, which looked like giving trouble, and were on the inter-company boundary. Just before reaching this position 2nd Lieut. D.B.S. BUXTON was wounded, and No.2. Company being without an Officer carried on to the second objective under their N.C.Os. until 2nd Lieut. F.H. MARTIN took command of No.2. Company.

Preparations were being made to outflank VEE BEND when the garrison surrendered, and thirty five prisoners with three machine guns gave themselves up to two Sergeants who had worked round the flank, so the advance was continued to the second objective which was reached at about 8.15 a.m. The line was consolidated under cover of the barrage, and three quarters of an hour afterwards the 3rd Bn. Coldstream Guards went through to take the third objective.

The total captures of the Battalion were found to be 1 Officer, and about 100 Other Ranks, and ten machine guns, also a good many of the enemy had been killed or wounded.

In the evening of the 9th, Nos.1. & 3. Companies were withdrawn from the line, and in the night 10th/11th Nos.2. & 4. Companies were relieved

Sheet No.4.

by the 4th Bn. Grenadier Guards.

The Medical Officer was wounded early in the day, and it was impossible to replace him. Great difficulty was experienced in clearing the wounded as the going was so bad, and the "carry" so long, but full use was made of the prisoners.

During the action the Battalion lost:-

	Killed.	Died of Wounds.	Wounded.	Missing.	Total.
Officers.	1.	1.	4.	-	6.
Other Ranks.	40.	-	117.	23.	180.

(Sd) G.B.S. FOLLETT

Lieut.-Colonel,
Commanding,
2nd Battalion Coldstream Guards.

12. 10. 1917.

WAR DIARY or INTELLIGENCE SUMMARY.

Army Form C. 2118.

2 Bn Coldstream Gds
November 1917

VA 38

Place	Date	Hour	Summary of Events and Information	Remarks and references to Appendices
In the Field.	Nov. 1st.		LA COMMUNE (Training).	
	2nd.		— do —	
	3rd.		— do —	
	4th.		— do —	
	5th.		— do —	
	6th.		— do — Lieut: J.H.MANSFIELD joined.	
	7th.		— do —	
	8th.		— do —	
	9th.		— do —	
	10th.		— do —	
	11th.		The Battalion paraded at 8.15 a.m. and proceeded by march route to INGHEM via MOULLE — ST.MARTIN — WIZERNES — GRAND BOIS. arriving about 4.30 p.m.	
	12th.		The Battalion paraded at 8.15 a.m. and proceeded by march route to LIVOSSART via THEROUANNE — ENQUINE GATTE — EQUIN les MINES — CUHEM-LAIRES arriving at 12.45 p.m.	
	13th.		The Battalion paraded at 9 a.m. and proceeded by march route to MONCHY BRETON via FIEFS — TANGRY — VALHOUN — LA THIEULOYE arriving at 2 p.m.	
	14th.		Billets at MONCHY BRETON.	
	15th.		— do — Overcoats and Surplus kit were dumped at ST.POL.	

Army Form C. 2118.

WAR DIARY
or
INTELLIGENCE SUMMARY.
(Erase heading not required.)

Instructions regarding War Diaries and Intelligence Summaries are contained in F. S. Regs., Part II. and the Staff Manual respectively. Title pages will be prepared in manuscript.

Place	Date	Hour	Summary of Events and Information	Remarks and references to Appendices
In the Field.	Nov. 16th		Billets at MONCHY BRETON.	
	17th.		The Battalion paraded at 8.40 a.m. and proceeded by march route to LINGEREUIL via CHELERS – TINGUES – PENIN – GIVENCHY les NOBLE arriving about midday.	
	18th.		The Battalion proceeded by march route to BLAIREVILLE Area via HAUTEVILLE – WANQUETIN – SIMENCOURT – BRETENCOURT arriving at 3.30 p.m. Guards Reinforcement Battalion at BUS les ARTOIS formed.	
	19th		The Battalion paraded at 5.30 p.m. and marched via HENDECOURT – BOISEUX au MONT – HAMELINCOURT – ERVILLERS to GOMIECOURT arriving at 10.30 p.m.	
	20th.		Camp near GOMIECOURT.	
	21st.		The Battalion paraded at 5.30 p.m. and marched to HAMELINCOURT where they embussed for BARASTRE arriving in camp about 11 p.m.	
	22nd		Camp near BARASTRE	

WAR DIARY
or
INTELLIGENCE SUMMARY.

(Erase heading not required.)

Army Form C. 2118.

Place	Date	Hour	Summary of Events and Information	Remarks and references to Appendices
In the Field.	Nov. 23rd.		At 5 a.m. the 1st Guards Brigade marched from BARASTRE and arrived at DOIGNIES about 10.30 a.m. where they bivouacked in the mud and had dinners. At 4.30 p.m. orders were received to dump all surplus kit and be ready to move. At 7.15 p.m. the whole Brigade marched out of DOIGNIES with orders to relieve the 152nd Infantry Brigade who were holding the line opposite FONTAINE and came into IV Corps. The route was through DEMICOURT and along the track to cross the Canal at K.9.b. The whole of the transport was ordered to follow the Battalions. It soon became evident that the track was impassable for transport and the very greatest difficulty was experienced in getting the wagons along and on arrival at the Canal bank orders were received that all transport was to be sent back and move round the West and South of HAVRINCOURT Wood to RIBECOURT. By this time horses and men were exhausted so they outspanned and remained where they were for the night. Meanwhile the head of the Brigade was still halted at the West bank of the Canal waiting for guides. The Brigadier was not with the Brigade having left DOIGNIES at 2.30 p.m. to reconnoitre the line, so touch with him was completely lost. The Commanding Officer was therefore temporarily in command of the Brigade and went forward to GRAINCOURT to find the Headquarters of the 119th Infantry Brigade and to try and get in touch with the Brigadier and to find the guides. The guides were found in GRAINCOURT and had been given a wrong map reference to meet the Brigade.	
do.	Nov. 24th		At 12.30 a.m. the guides were brought back to the Brigade and the march was resumed via GRAINCOURT and LA JUSTICE Cross-roads in L.l.d. The 1st Battn. Irish Guards, 2nd Battn. Grenadier Guards, and 3rd Battn. Coldstream Guards relieved the front line, and the 2nd Battn. Coldstream Guards relieved parts of the 6th Gordons and 6th Seaforths in the support line along the road with the left on the Cross-roads at L.l.d. and the right in L.9.c. At 5.30 a.m. the relief was completed and by this time all ranks were completely exhausted having been marching for 23 hours with a 7 hours halt in the middle. This completed a record relief in this war, so much so that the Headquarters 51st Division were so convinced that it was impossible for the 1st Guards Brigade to carry out the relief two sets of orders were issued Scheme A & B, a copy of Scheme A orders by the 152nd Infantry	

Army Form C. 2118.

WAR DIARY
or
INTELLIGENCE SUMMARY.
(Erase heading not required.)

Instructions regarding War Diaries and Intelligence Summaries are contained in F. S. Regs., Part II. and the Staff Manual respectively. Title pages will be prepared in manuscript.

Place	Date	Hour	Summary of Events and Information	Remarks and references to Appendices
In the Field.	Nov. 24th (continued)		Brigade is attached.	
do.	Nov. 25th.		A quiet day in support and at 5 p.m. No. 4 Coy. went up into BOURLON WOOD to reinforce the 3rd Guards Brigade. 3/4 Coldstream Guards	
do.	Nov. 26th.		After a quiet day the Battalion was relieved at 7 p.m. by the 1st Battalion Coldstream Guards and marched back to bivouac in the old No Mans Land S.W. of RIBECOURT about Q.5.d. and came into Divisional Reserve. The casualties for the tour were 5 wounded.	
do.	Nov. 27th		At 6 p.m. Nos. 1, 2 & 3 Coys. with Battn. Headquarters went up to BOURLON WOOD in support. No. 4 Coy. and the details marched to METZ to billets.	
do.	Nov. 28th.		At 7 p.m. the three Coys. and Battn. H.Q. were relieved by the 2/6th South Staffords 59th Division and marched back to bivouac having had 29 killed and wounded, and B/Lieut: R.O.C.DRUMMOND killed.	
do.	Nov. 29th.		At 2 a.m. Battn. Headquarters and Nos. 1, 2 & 3 Coys. reached the billeting area at Q.5.d and at mid-day marched to METZ.	
do.	Nov. 30th		See report of operations attached.	

December 8th 1917.

signature
Lieut Colonel.
Commanding,
2nd Battalion Coldstream Guards.

2nd Battalion Coldstream Guards.

Account of Operations 30th November - 1st December 1917.
Reference Map GOUZEAUCOURT 1/20,000.

On 29th November 1917 the 2nd Battalion Coldstream Guards moved into METZ-EN-COUTURE on coming out of BOURLON WOOD, and spent the night of 29/30th November under the little cover that could be found in the ruins of the village. The men were very tired after their strenuous exertions during the last few days. Soon after a late breakfast on the 30th November the Battalion received orders to be ready to move at three-quarters of an hour's notice because the Germans had launched powerful attacks against the southern face of the salient. This was immediately followed at 11.15 a.m. by all Battalions of the 1st Guards Brigade being ordered to parade at once. The Brigadier had already ridden on to reconnoitre the position and Commanding Officers were ordered to follow him towards GOUZEAUCOURT as soon as possible. The situation appeared to be very grave as the roads were blocked by every description of vehicles in flight and men were streaming back along the roads and across country without arms or equipment in disorganized mobs.

On reaching GOUZEAUCOURT WOOD it was evident that the Germans were in possession of GOUZEAUCOURT.

The Brigadier decided to counter-attack at once to retake GOUZEAUCOURT and gain the high ridge East of that village, known as QUENTIN Ridge.

The METZ - GOUZEAUCOURT road gave the direction of the attack and the Brigade was ordered to attack as follows :- 1st Battn. Irish Guards on the left North of the road, the 3rd Battn. Coldstream Guards in the centre on the South of the road and the 2nd Battalion Coldstream Guards on the right. The 2nd Battn. Grenadier Guards were to remain in Brigade Reserve East of GOUZEAUCOURT Wood.

On arrival the Battalion wheeled off the road into the clearing in Q.28.c. under cover of the ridge and after unloading the Lewis Guns got into position as follows :-
No. 4 Coy. on the right under Lieut: W.G.OAKMAN with 2/Lieuts:
F.H.MARTIN and A.H.G.BUTCHER.

No. 1 Coy. on the left under Captain H.C.St.J.THOMPSON with
    Captain W.A.C.WILKINSON and Lieuts: G.C.FIRBANK and I.LAING.

No. 2 Coy. supporting No. 4 Coy. under Captain F.W.BUTLER-THWING with
    Lieut: W.B.ST.LEGER.

No. 3 Coy. supporting No. 1 Coy. under Captain H.J.R.BRIERLY with
    2/Lieut: A.J.C.A.BUGLER.

Each of the leading Companies had a frontage of 200 yards with two platoons in the first wave and two platoons in the rear wave. The supporting Companies were in the same formation.

By 12.30 p.m. the remaining Battalions of the Brigade were reported to be in position and the attack commenced. At this moment a message was received stating that the 3rd Guards Brigade were coming up on the right to attack also. The Adjutant, Captain J.S.COATS went on his horse some distance to endeavour to get in touch with the 3rd Guards Brigade and failed to do so. It was afterwards discovered that the orders for the 3rd Guards Brigade had been cancelled and they were ordered to move round through METZ and come up on the left of the 1st Guards Brigade.

The earlier stages of the attack were without incident beyond a good deal of shelling both shrapnel and H.E. but on reaching the top of the crest heavy machine gun fire was opened on the leading lines.

It was at this point that the most wonderful spectacle presented itself - away to the left as far as the eye could reach, the Brigade could be seen advancing in four waves in perfect formation as if they were carrying out an Aldershot Field Day, advancing by rushes, nothing could stop them except when three belts of barbed wire in front of the British reserve trenches had to be cut through.

It was on the right that the chief anxiety lay, as, so far, it was in the air, but to meet any opposition from that quarter, the sub-sections of the 1st Guards Brigade M.G. Coy. was distributed with one Gun on the right and one in the centre of the leading wave and two guns behind the Battalion's right rear.

On getting within a thousand yards of the Western edge of the village it was found that a few R.E. had gallantly hung on to a trench and had held up the enemy's advance on the right front, also elements of the 29th Division began to come up on the right and a little later the 20th Hussars of the 5th Cavalry Brigade came up and fell in on our right to attack dismounted.

On going down the slope towards the village, the German machine gun fire became intense but this only spurred the Brigade on to go faster, and the four lines went down the steep hill and up the slopes towards the village a tremendous pace, and the Germans could be seen clearing out of the village to the West in considerable numbers.

The line of the attack brought the left of the Battalion on to the cross-roads in Q.36.c. so the whole Battalion had to attack over the high ridge South of the village which brought them under direct observation of the German artillery on QUENTIN Ridge.

The Germans took full advantage of this and put down a heavy barrage with 5.9 cm. 7.7 cm. and captured British field guns, causing many casualties, and the Germans who had retired from GOUZEAUCOURT had taken up a position in one of the British trenches about 600 yards East of the railway and were also holding the railway.

By 1.30 p.m. the whole village was in our hands and the attack was pressing forward down the slopes on the Eastern side to take QUENTIN ridge.

It was going down this slope that Captain H.C.St.J.THOMPSON was wounded and died soon afterwards, so his place was taken by Captain W.A.C.WILKINSON who was immediately hit also but carried on to the end, and Lieut: LAING was killed.

In No. 2 Coy. Captain F.W.BUTLER-THWING was hit and Lieut: W.B.ST.LEGER being the only Officer left took command of the Company.

In No. 4 Coy. Lieut: W.G.OAKMAN and 2/Lieut: A.H.G.BUTCHER were

wounded
/leaving 2/Lieut: F.H.MARTIN alone to command the Company.
No. 1 Coy. had not had any casualties in their Officers.
On reaching the foot of the slope the leading lines found the sunken road running through W.6.c. and dug in on that line.
No. 2 Coy. had reinforced No. 4 Coy.
The men were very exhausted, and the hostile opposition too strong to attempt any further advance without some support, so No. 3 Coy. dug in supporting the front line half way down the slope.

At 2.45 p.m. a cavalry regiment came into action mounted on our right and made a gallant attempt to turn the enemy's left but were prevented from doing so by wire and were heavily fired on by machine guns and artillery.

At 3.30 p.m. eleven tanks came up from the right rear with orders to retake GOUZEAUCOURT which had already been taken by that time, so they in their turn became the target of the German artillery and were pounded by salvoes of 5.9 in. Howitzers and four tanks were soon put out of action and left in flames, but the crews most gallantly got their Lewis Guns out and fell in with the Battalion to meet any counter-attack.

By this time it began to get dark and the battle died down, both sides being exhausted.

This gave the opportunity of looking round to see the results of the battle. GOUZEAUCOURT village was found to be full of British guns that the Brigade had retaken - there was a 12 inch howitzer and many 8 inch and 6 inch, not to mention enormous dumps of ammunition of all kinds and war material.

The right Companies of the 2nd Battalion Coldstream Guards had retaken a supply train loaded with supplies which was most useful as there had been no time to issue rations before the attack began and this train load fed the whole Brigade for the next 48 hours. Luckily the Germans had not had sufficient time to destroy anything but had looted a good deal, as every German dead and wounded was found to have supplemented his own rations by a loaf of white bread. All these German rations were collected by men detailed from Battalion Headquarters and were very useful.

It was found also that the Germans had ripped open the mail bags and acres of ground were strewn with broken parcels and letters. Everyone was now very hungry having had nothing to eat all day and the curious spectacle presented itself of men of every branch of the service walking about eating mince-pies and cakes that were lying about on the ground in great profusion.

The night of 30th November/1st December was luckily very quiet and many guns were got out of the village by tractors, and a good line was dug covering the sunken road so that by dawn on the 1st December No. 2 Coy. on the right, No. 4 Coy. in the centre and No. 1 Coy. on the left had dug a continuous trench and were in touch with the cavalry on the right, who had been reinforced by 3 Coys. of Middlesex from 20th Division, and with the 3rd Battalion Coldstream Guards on the left.

The greatest credit is due to all ranks for the way they dug during the night as they had nothing but the entrenching tool to dig with.

The casualty reports that came in during the night showed that the attack had been costly; out of eleven Company Officers two were killed and FOUR wounded; in O.R's there were 235 killed, wounded and missing.

At 6.20 a.m. on 1st December the 2nd Battn. Grenadier Guards went through the 2nd Battn. Coldstream Guards to attack the QUENTIN Ridge in conjunction with the cavalry on the right and the 3rd Battn. Coldstream Guards on the left. The 2nd Battn. Coldstream Guards therefore remained in their positions and became supports and were heavily shelled all day.

At 5 p.m. No. 3 Coy. under Captain H.J.L.BRIERLY went up to protect the right of the 2nd Battn. Grenadier Guards in GAUCHE WOOD.

At 8 p.m. the Battalion was relieved by the 2nd Battalion Irish Guards and went back into reserve in GOUZEAUCOURT WOOD.

This ended the operations in so far as it affected the 2nd Battn. Coldstream Guards.

It is only fair to the men engaged in the battle to say that never has the Brigade of Guards done such a magnificent performance in the whole of its history.

The attack not only regained a bit of lost ground but saved the whole of the 3rd Army from utter disaster. This is evidently realized by the Higher Commands judging by the numerous and highly complimentary messages that were received by the G.O.C. 1st Guards Brigade.

The gallant few, consisting of elements of R.E., of Infantry and of Labour Battalions who had hung on to the high ground S.W. of GOUZEAUCOURT were relieved beyond words to see the 1st Guards Brigade coming up on their left, and the greatest compliment of all came from an old Sapper who was so overcome by the spectacle of the Brigade attacking that he turned to the Battalion Medical Officer and said with tears in his eyes that "there was no bloody shit on earth that could stop them fucking Guards".

Copy of a letter received from The Corps Commander III Corps.

" The Corps Commander wishes to express to all ranks of the Guards Division his high appreciation of the prompt manner in which they turned out on the 30th November, counter-attacked through a disorganized rabble and retook GOUZEAUCOURT. The very fine attack which they subsequently carried out against QUENTIN RIDGE and GAUCHE WOOD, resulting in the capture of these important positions, was worthy of the highest traditions of the Guards.

I shall be much obliged if you will furnish me with the names of any Officers, N.C.O's and men who distinguished themselves on this occasion."

9.12.17.

G.10/121.

Officers Commanding
5th Seaforth Highs.
6th Seaforth Highs.
6th Gordon Highlds.
8th A. & S. Highs.
152nd M. G. Company.

9th Royal Scots.
7th Black Watch.
4th Gordon Highs.
===============================

1.   The 1st Guards Brigade has marched twenty miles today and will probably arrive very fatigued. The B.G.C. wishes all ranks to realise the importance of handing over good trenches and fire positions in order to save the 1st Guards Brigade as much digging as possible.

2.   In the event of Scheme A coming into force -

2nd Grenadier Guards will take over A Sector.
1st Irish Guards will take over B Sector.
3rd Coldstream Guards will take over C Sector.
2nd Coldstream Guards will be in reserve.

(Sgd) N.B. GIBBS.

Captain, Brigade Major,
152nd Infantry Brigade.

23rd Nov. 1917.

WAR DIARY
or
INTELLIGENCE SUMMARY.

(Erase heading not required.)

Army Form C. 2118.

Place	Date	Hour	Summary of Events and Information	Remarks and references to Appendices
In the Field.	Dec. 1st 1917.		Trenches near GOUZEAUCOURT. On relief by the 2nd Battalion Irish Guards the Battalion marched to bivouacs in GOUZEAUCOURT WOOD. (Casualties:- O.R. 3 Killed 1 Wounded)	
	2nd		GOUZEAUCOURT WOOD. (Bivouacs).	
	3rd.		--do-- Battalion paraded at 5.30 p.m. and relieved the 4th Battalion Grenadier Guards in the trenches GONNELIEU - VILLERS-GUISLAIN Line (Quentin Ridge).	
	4th		Trenches (Quentin Ridge). On relief by the 3rd Battalion Coldstream Guards the Battalion marched back to bivouacs in GOUZEAUCOURT WOOD.	
	5th.		GOUZEAUCOURT WOOD. (Bivouacs). On relief by the 8th Battalion Black Watch the Battalion paraded at 6 p.m. and marched to billets in METZ-en-COUTURE.	
	6th.		METZ-en-COUTURE. The Battalion paraded at 8 a.m. and marched via FINS - EUANCOURT - to ETRICOURT Siding where it entrained for BEAUMETZ-les-LOGES, thence marching to camp at BERNEVILLE.	
	7th to 19th.		Camp at BERNEVILLE (Reorganization and Training).	
	20th		--do-- The following O.R's were awarded the MILITARY MEDAL in connection with the operations of November 25th-28th.1917. No. 12745. Pte T.CONNEIL. No. 17363. Pte. E.G.MANKTELOW. 15377. " G.MEDFORTH. 15225. " W.COATES.	
	21st to 31st		Camp at BERNEVILLE (Reorganization and Training).	

January 3rd 1917.

S.M....... Major.
Commanding,
2nd Battalion Coldstream Guards.

WAR DIARY or INTELLIGENCE SUMMARY.

(Erase heading not required.)

Army Form C. 2118.

1st Bde. January 1, 1918.
2nd Bn Coldstream Gds.

Vol 40

Place	Date	Hour	Summary of Events and Information	Remarks and references to Appendices
	Jan. 1st 1918.		Camp at BERNEVILLE (Training). A list of various Honours & Awards published this day is attached.	
	2nd.		The Battalion paraded at 1.30 p.m. and marched via WARLUS - DAINVILLE to billets in ARRAS (Rue d'Amiens), arriving about 3 p.m.	
	3rd. 4th. 5th. 6th. 7th. 8th.		Billets in ARRAS (Training). ditto. ditto. ditto. ditto. ditto. Notification was received of the grant of the MILITARY CROSS to Captain & Adjutant J.S.Coats. Captain C.Sutton-Nelthorpe and 2/Lieut: G.B.Heath joined the Battalion.	
	9th.		Billets in ARRAS (Training).	
	10th.		The Battalion paraded at 4 p.m. and entrained at "Q" Dump (G.21.b.8.7. - Sheet 51B.N.W.) detraining at H.22.d.8.4. and relieving the 1st Battalion Coldstream Guards in the left sector of the Brigade front.	
	11th. 12th. 13th. 14th.		Trenches. (Casualties - 2 O.R. Killed, 1 O.R. Wounded) do. do. On relief by the 3rd Battalion Coldstream Guards the Battalion marched back to trenches near FAMPOUX and came into Brigade reserve.	
	15th.		Reserve Trenches.	
	16th.		ditto. (Casualties - 1 O.R. Killed, 4 O.R. Wounded).	
	17th.		Reserve trenches.	
			(Continued.)	

Army Form C. 2118.

WAR DIARY
or
INTELLIGENCE SUMMARY.

(Erase heading not required.)

Instructions regarding War Diaries and Intelligence Summaries are contained in F. S. Regs., Part II. and the Staff Manual respectively. Title pages will be prepared in manuscript.

Place	Date	Hour	Summary of Events and Information	Remarks and references to Appendices
	Jan. 18th 1918.		The Battalion relieved the 3rd Battalion Coldstream Guards in the left sector of the Brigade front.	
	19th		Trenches.	
	20th		do. A list of various Honours & Awards published this day is attached.	
	21st		do. Battn.Hd.Qrs &	
	22nd		On relief by the 3rd Battalion Coldstream Guards/Nos. 3 & 4 Companies marched back to billets in ARRAS, (Rue Frederick Degeorges), and Nos. 1 & 2 Companies marched to trenches near FAMPOUX. The Battalion now came into Brigade Reserve.	
	23rd.		Battn.Hd.Qrs. & Nos. 3 & 4 Coys - billets in ARRAS, Nos. 1 & 2 Coys in trenches.	
	24th.		- do - - do -	
	25th.		- do - - do -	
	26th.		Battn.Hd.Qrs, & Nos. 3 & 4 Coys. paraded at 4.15 p.m. and marched to billets in the Rue d'Amiens, ARRAS. On relief by the 2nd Battn. Scots Guards Nos. 1 & 2 Coys. entrained to "Q" Dump and marched to join the remainder of the Battalion.	
	27th.		Billets in ARRAS (Training).	
	28th.		ditto.	
	29th.		ditto.	
	30th.		ditto.	
	31st.		ditto.	
	February 1st 1918.			

Major,
Commanding.
2nd Battalion Coldstream Guards.

HONOURS & AWARDS.   January 1st 1918.

BAR TO THE MILITARY CROSS.

Lieut. (a/Capt.) W.A.C.WILKINSON, M.C.

THE MILITARY CROSS.

Lieut: (a/Capt.) H.J.R.BRIERLY.
2/Lieut: A.H.G.BUTCHER.
Lieut: C.J.B.SYMON.
Lieut: G.C.FIRBANK.
2/Lieut: F.H.MARTIN.

THE DISTINGUISHED CONDUCT MEDAL.

No. 5635. Sgt. S.J.THURSFIELD.
    7181. C.S.Major C.W.RYMAN.
    6906. Pte. J.W.HARRIS.

THE MILITARY CROSS.

T/Capt. P.H.WELLS. R.A.M.C.   attached 2nd Bn. Coldstream Gds.

HONOURS & AWARDS.   January 20th 1918.

THE MILITARY MEDAL.

No. 8858. L/Cpl. W.HARRISON.
   12007. Pte.   E.O.STADDON.
   15521. L/Cpl. E.CROOKES.
    7803. C.Q.M.S.(a/C.S.M.) A.D.SINCLAIR.
   20016. Pte.   J.WEST.
   11610. "   H.W.WILSON.
    9774. Sergt. O.W.BATTRICK.
   10072. Pte.   W.R.NUTTALL.
    5112. Sergt. G.OSBORNE.
   11926. Corpl.(L/Sgt).J.HUDGELL.
    9260.   "   "   T.W.CARTER.
   13127. Pte.   T.BENSON.
   12168. "   W.J.GARRARD.
    8492. Corpl.(L/Sgt) E.FERGUSON.

WAR DIARY
INTELLIGENCE SUMMARY.

(Erase heading not required.)

Army Form C. 2118.

February 1, 1918.

2nd Bn. Coldstream Gds.

Vol 41

Place	Date	Hour	Summary of Events and Information	Remarks and references to Appendices
In the Field.	Feb. 1st. 1918.		Billets in ARRAS. Training.	
	2nd.		The Battalion paraded about 4.30 p.m. and marched to "Q" Dump, ARRAS, thence entraining to FAMPOUX Station, arriving about 6 p.m. The Battalion then marched to the Front Line trenches, relieving parts of the 1st & 2nd Battalions Scots Guards. The front taken over by the Battalion was a new Sector allotted to the 1st Guards Brigade.	
	3rd.		Front Line Trenches.	
	4th.		do.	
	5th.		do. (Casualty - 1 O.R. wounded)	
	6th.		The Battalion was relieved by the 2nd Battalion Grenadier Guards about 8 p.m. and marched back to FAMPOUX Station, thence entraining to "Q" Dump and marching to billets in the PRISON, ARRAS. A draft of 94 O.R. joined the Battalion.	
	7th.		PRISON, ARRAS. Training.	
	8th.		do. do.	
	9th.		do. do.	
	10th.		The Battalion paraded about 5 p.m. and marched to "Q" Dump, ARRAS, thence entraining to FAMPOUX Station, and marching to the Support Line Trenches, relieving the 1st Battalion Irish Guards.	
	11th.		Support Line Trenches. Fatigues.	
	12th.		do. do.	
	13th.		do. do. 2/Lieut: G.C.L.Atkinson joined the Battn.	
	14th.		The Battalion was relieved by the 2nd Battalion Grenadier Guards about 5.45 p.m. and marched to the Front Line Trenches relieving the 1st Battn. Irish Guards. Continued.	

Army Form C. 2118.

WAR DIARY
INTELLIGENCE SUMMARY.

(Erase heading not required.)

Instructions regarding War Diaries and Intelligence Summaries are contained in F.S. Regs., Part II and the Staff Manual respectively. Title pages will be prepared in manuscript.

Place	Date	Hour	Summary of Events and Information	Remarks and references to Appendices
In the Field.	Feb. 15th. 1918.		Front Line Trenches. (Casualties 1 O.R. Killed & 1 O.R. Wounded)	
	16th		do. (Casualty - 1 O.R. Killed)	
	17th		do.	
	18th		The Battalion was relieved about 7 p.m. by the 2nd Battalion Grenadier Guards and marched back to GORDON Camp, near BLANGY. Draft of 40 O.R. joined Battalion.	
	19th. 20th 21st		GORDON Camp. Training. do. do. do. do.	
	22nd		The Battalion paraded at 5.30 p.m. and proceeded by march route to the Support Line Trenches, relieving the 1st Battalion Irish Guards. 2/Lt S.M. Crichton and 2/Lt Geoff Taylor joined + Draft of 2 O.R.	
	23rd. 24th 25th		Support Line Trenches. Draft 6 O.R. joined do. do.	
	26th.		The Battalion paraded about 5.45 p.m. and marched to the Front Line trenches, relieving the 1st Battn. Irish Guards.	
	27th. 28th		Front Line trenches. Casualties - O.R. W.1. (remaining at duty). do. Casualties - O.R. W. 2)	
March 1st 1918.				

S.M.M. Clok
Lieut-Colonel.
Commanding,
2nd Battalion Coldstream Guards.

Army Form C. 2118.

WAR DIARY

INTELLIGENCE SUMMARY

(Erase heading not required.)

Instructions regarding War Diaries and Intelligence Summaries are contained in F. S. Regs. Part II. and the Staff Manual respectively. Title pages will be prepared in manuscript.

Place	Date	Hour	Summary of Events and Information	Remarks and references to Appendices
In the Field	March 1st 1918.		Front line trenches. Casualties 2 other ranks wounded.	
	2nd.		The Battalion was relieved by the 2nd Battalion Grenadier Guards and entrained at FAMPOUX, detraining at "Q" Dump, ARRAS, thence proceeding to billets in the PRISON, ARRAS.	
	3rd.		PRISON, ARRAS. (Training). 2/Lieut: L.W.G. Eccles, M.C. joined the Battalion.	
	4th.		—do— —do— —do—	
	5th.		—do— —do— —do—	
	6th.		The Battalion paraded at 4-30p.m. and proceeded by march-route to the Support Line, relieving the 1st Battalion Irish Guards. Casualties 1 other rank killed, 4 other ranks wounded.	
	7th.		Support Line Trenches.	
	8th.		—do—. Casualties 1 other rank wounded.	
	9th.		—do—.	
	10th.		The Battalion paraded at 7-20p.m. and relieved the 1st Battalion Irish Guards in the Front Line.	
	11th.		Front Line Trenches.	
	12th.		—do—	
	13th.		—do— Casualties 6 other ranks wounded.	
	14th.		The Battalion was relieved by the 2nd Battalion Grenadier Guards and proceeded by march-route to STIRLING CAMP arriving about 10-30p.m.	
			continued:—	

Army Form C. 2118.

WAR DIARY
or
INTELLIGENCE SUMMARY.

(Erase heading not required.)

Instructions regarding War Diaries and Intelligence Summaries are contained in F. S. Regs., Part II. and the Staff Manual respectively. Title pages will be prepared in manuscript.

Place	Date	Hour	Summary of Events and Information	Remarks and references to Appendices
In the Field.	March 15th 1918.		STIRLING CAMP. (Training).	
	16th		—do—	
	17th		—do—	
	18th		The Battalion paraded at 7p.m. and proceeded by march-route relieving the 1st Battalion Irish Guards in the Support Line. Casualties 1 other rank killed, 5 other ranks wounded.	
	19th		Support Line Trenches.	
	20th		The Battalion was relieved by the 1st Battalion Hampshire Regiment and entrained at ATHIES, detraining at "Q" Dump, ARRAS and proceeding by march-route to billets in SCHRAMM BARRACKS, ARRAS.	
	21st		SCHRAMM BARRACKS. (CORPS RESERVE). Casualties 1 other rank wounded.	
	22nd		The Battalion paraded about 10-30p.m. and proceeded by march-route to BOISLEUX-au-MONT and Dug in in Support. 2/Lieut: W. Jackson and 65 other ranks joined the Battalion. Lieut:-Colonel G.B.S. Follett D.S.O.,M.V.O., left the Battalion to Command the 2nd Guards Brigade. Casualties 1 other rank wounded.	
	23rd.		Support Trenches near BOISLEUX-au-MONT. Casualties 1 other rank wounded.	
	24th		The Battalion withdrew to a new Support Line near BOIRY-ST.MARTIN. Casualties 4 O.R. Killed 13 O.R. Wounded.	
	25th		Support Line near BOIRY-ST.MARTIN. Casualties 1 O.R. Wounded	

Army Form C. 2118.

WAR DIARY or INTELLIGENCE SUMMARY.

(Erase heading not required.)

Instructions regarding War Diaries and Intelligence Summaries are contained in F. S. R. gs., Part II. and the Staff Manual respectively. Title pages will be prepared in manuscript.

Place	Date	Hour	Summary of Events and Information	Remarks and references to Appendices
In the Field.	March 26th 1918.		The Battalion paraded at 9 p.m. and relieved the 3rd Battalion Grenadier Guards in support near MOYENNEVILLE. Casualties 5/O.R. Killed 25/O.R. Wounded 1 O.R. Missing.	
	27th.		Support near MOYENNEVILLE. Casualties 5 O.R. Killed, 20 O.R. Wounded 1 O.R. Missing.	
	28th.		— do. — 2/Lieut: F.H.MARTIN M.C. and 3 O.R. Killed, 7 O.R. Wounded.	
	29th.		— do. — Casualties 1 O.R. Killed 2 O.R. Wounded.	
	30th.		The Battalion was relieved by the 2nd & 3rd Battns. Grenadier Guards and 1st Battn. Irish Guards, proceeded by march-route to camp near HENDECOURT, becoming the Battalion in Reserve. Casualties 1 O.R. Killed, 6 O.R. Wounded. Lt.C.E.ESPIN and 2/Lt.E.J.Fitzgerald joined Battalion.	
	31st.		Camp near HENDECOURT. Casualties 3 O.R. Wounded.	
	April 10th 1918.			

E.P.Feney,
Major,
Commanding,
2nd Battalion Coldstream Guards.

Guards Division.
1st Guards Brigade

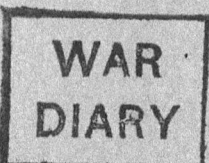

2nd BATTALION

THE COLDSTREAM GUARDS

APRIL 1918

WAR DIARY
or
INTELLIGENCE SUMMARY.

(Erase heading not required.)

Army Form C. 2118.

April, 1918

2nd Bn Coldstream Guards

96 43

Place	Date	Hour	Summary of Events and Information	Remarks and references to Appendices
Camp near HENDECOURT (Reserve)	April 1st 1918.		Casualties - 2 O.R.Killed, 11 O.R.Wounded.	
	2nd		The Battalion paraded at 9 p.m. and relieved portions of the 2nd & 3rd Battns. Grenadier Guards in the right Battalion Sector of the Brigade Front. (Casualties - 1 O.R.Killed) Lieut: H.L.Farquhar & 2/Lieut: W.R.Scott and Draft of 22 O.R. joined Battalion.	
Front Line trenches.	3rd		Casualties - 1 O.R.Wounded.	
Front Line trenches.	4th			
	5th		The Battalion was relieved by the 1st Battn. Irish Guards and proceeded to a camp near HENDECOURT, becoming the Battalion in reserve. Casualties - 4 O.R.Wounded.	
Camp near HENDECOURT (Reserve).	6th		Casualties - 1 O.R.Wounded. Draft of 36 O.R. Joined Battn.	
	7th		The Battalion paraded at 8.30 p.m. and relieved the 2nd Battn. Grenadier Guards in the left Battalion Sector of the Brigade Front. Casualties 1 O.R.Killed, 12 O.B.Wounded.	
Front Line trenches.	8th		Casualties-3 O.R.Killed, 14 O.R.Wounded.	
Front Line trenches.	9th		Casualties - 9 O.R.Wounded.	
Front Line trenches.	10th		Casualties - 1 O.R.Wounded.	
	11th		The Battalion was relieved at night by the 1st. Battn. Irish Guards and marched back to camp near HENDECOURT, becoming Battalion in Reserve. Casualties - 2 O.R.Wounded.	
Camp near HENDECOURT (Reserve)	12th		Casualties - 1 O.R.Killed, 1 O.R.Wounded.	
			continued.	

Army Form C. 2118.

WAR DIARY
or
INTELLIGENCE SUMMARY.

(Erase heading not required.)

Instructions regarding War Diaries and Intelligence Summaries are contained in F.S. Regs., Part II and the Staff Manual respectively. Title pages will be prepared in manuscript.

Place	Date	Hour	Summary of Events and Information	Remarks and references to Appendices
In the Field	April 13th		The Battalion was relieved about 8 p.m. by the 2nd Batt.n Oxford & Bucks. Light Infantry and proceeded by march-route to BAVINCOURT - via BLAIREVILLE, BRETENCOURT, BEAUMETZ-les-LOGES, Main road, BAVINCOURT, arriving in billets about 1 a.m. Draft of 22 O.R. joined Battalion.	
	14th		Billets in BAVINCOURT (Training)	
	15th		- do -	
	16th		- do - 1 O.R. Killed and 3 O.R. Injured accidentally through the collapse of some wire beds.	
	17th		- do -	
	18th		- do - Draft of 11 O.R. joined Battalion.	
	19th		- do -	
	20th		- do -	
	21st		- do - Draft of 3 O.R. joined Battalion.	
	22nd		- do -	
	23rd		- do -	
	24th		The Battalion paraded at 7 p.m. and marched to the main road where it embussed - proceeding via LA CAUCHIE - POMMIER, to debussing point at TOWER HOUSE. Guides were met and the Battalion relieved the 1st Batt.n. Dorset Regiment in the Right Sector of the Brigade Front. (1 O.R. Missing)	
	25th		Trenches near AYETTE. Casualties - 1 O.R. Wounded.	
			Continued.	

Army Form C. 2118.

WAR DIARY
or
INTELLIGENCE SUMMARY.
(Erase heading not required.)

Instructions regarding War Diaries and Intelligence Summaries are contained in F. S. Regs., Part II. and the Staff Manual respectively. Title pages will be prepared in manuscript.

Place	Date	Hour	Summary of Events and Information	Remarks and references to Appendices
In the Field.	April 26th		Trenches near AYETTE. Casualties 1 O.R. Wounded.	
	27th		-do- Lieut: W.B.St.Leger M.C. wd 2 O.R. Killed. 2/Lieut: E.J.Fitzgerald & 2 O.R. Wounded	
	28th		The Battalion was relieved by the 1st Battn. Irish Guards at night and proceeded to a camp near MONCHY-au-BOIS. Casualties — 2 O.R. Killed, 4 O.R. Wounded.	
	29th		Camp near MONCHY-au-BOIS. Draft of 18 O.R. joined Battalion.	
	30th		-do-	
	May 2nd 1918.			

Signed,
Lieut:Colonel,
Commanding,
2nd Battalion Coldstream Guards.

WAR DIARY
INTELLIGENCE SUMMARY

May, 1918
Army Form C. 2118.

2nd Battalion Grenadier Guards

Place	Date	Hour	Summary of Events and Information	Remarks and references to Appendices
In-the-Field.	May 1st.		MONCHY trenches (Reserve). The Battalion paraded at 7.30 p.m. and relieved the 2nd Battalion Grenadier Guards in the left Subsector of the Brigade Front.	
	2nd.		Front Line Trenches. AYETTE.	
	3rd.		--do-- Casualties. 2 Wounded. A draft of 4 O.R's joined the Battalion.	
	4th.		--do-- Casualties. 6 Wounded. A draft of 16 O.R's joined the Battalion.	
	5th.		--do--	
	6th.		--do-- Major J.BULLOUGH joined the Battalion. (Captain C.Suttch-Nelthorpe awarded the Military Cross.)	
	7th.		--do-- The Battalion was relieved by the 1st Battalion Irish Guards, and marched back to the trenches near MONCHY, becoming the Battalion in Reserve. Casualties. 3 Killed. 2 Wounded. Lieut: H.M.D.BARLOW wounded (remained at duty). 2/Lieut: O.C.KENCH and 2/Lieut: E.F.S.GRAHAM and draft of 10 O.R's joined the Battalion.	
	8th.		MONCHY trenches. (Reserve).	
	9th.		--do-- 2/Lieut: J.J.T.INMAN joined the Battalion.	
	10th.		--do-- The Battalion paraded at 8 p.m. and relieved the 2nd Battalion Grenadier Guards in the Right Subsector of the Brigade Front. Casualties 2 Wounded (remained at duty.)	
	11th.		Front Line Trenches. AYETTE. Casualties. 2 Wounded.	
	12th.		--do--	
	13th.		--do--	
	14th.		--do-- Casualties. 2 Killed. 1 Wounded.	

(continued).

Army Form C. 2118.

WAR DIARY
INTELLIGENCE SUMMARY

(Erase heading not required.)

Instructions regarding War Diaries and Intelligence Summaries are contained in F. S. Regs, Part II. and the Staff Manual respectively. Title pages will be prepared in manuscript.

Place	Date	Hour	Summary of Events and Information	Remarks and references to Appendices
In-the-Field.	May. 15th.		Front Line Trenches. AYETTE. Casualties. 3 Wounded.	
	16th.	—do—	The Battalion was relieved by the 1st Battalion Irish Guards and marched back to trenches near MONCHY, becoming the Battalion in Reserve.	
	17th.		MONCHY trenches. (Reserve).	
	18th.	—do—	—do— Casualties. 1 Wounded. A draft of 19 O.R's joined the Battalion.	
	19th.	—do—	—do— The Battalion paraded at 8.30 p.m. and relieved the 2nd Battalion Grenadier Guards in the Left Subsector of the Brigade Front. Lieut: O.J.HAMBRO, M.C, and 2/Lieut: R.F.GOAD joined the Battalion.	
	20th.		Front Line Trenches. AYETTE. Casualties. 2 Wounded.	
	21st.	—do—	—do—	
	22nd.	—do—	—do— 2/Lieut: G.B.HEATH Wounded. Casualties. 1 Killed. 4 Wounded. 2/Lieut; F.G.Taylor joined the Battalion. A raid was carried out by No 1 Company on the night of the 22/23rd. An account of the operation is attached.	Appendix.
	23rd.	—do—	—do— Casualties. 7 Wounded. A draft of 4 O.R's joined the Battalion.	
	24th.	—do—	—do— Casualties. 1 Wounded.	
	25th.	—do—	—do— The Battalion was relieved by the 1st Battalion Irish Guards and marched back to trenches near MONCHY, becoming the Battalion in Reserve.	
	26th.		MONCHY trenches. (Reserve).	
	27th.	—do—	—do— Casualties. 4 Killed. 4 Wounded.	
	28th.	—do—	—do— The Battalion paraded at 8.30 p.m. and relieved the 2nd Battalion Grenadier Guards in the right Subsector of the Brigade Front.	
			(continued).	

Army Form C. 2118.

WAR DIARY
INTELLIGENCE SUMMARY
(Erase heading not required.)

Instructions regarding War Diaries and Intelligence
Summaries are contained in F. S. Regs., Part II.
and the Staff Manual respectively. Title pages
will be prepared in manuscript.

Place	Date	Hour	Summary of Events and Information	Remarks and references to Appendices
In-the-Field.	May 29th.		Front Line Trenches. AYETTE.	
	30th.		—do—	
	31st.		—do—	
			The undermentioned were awarded the MILITARY MEDAL in connection with the operations on the night of the 22/23rd May 1918.	
			No. 6952 Pte (L/Cpl) BRUFORD. S. No. 20724 Pte (L/Cpl) PLANT. G.J. No. 21672 Pte HUGHES. T.H. No. 18219 Pte MALLETT. W. No. 18709 Pte GREEN. W.H.	
	1st June 1918.			

Lieut: Colonel,
Commanding,
2nd. Battalion Coldstream Guards.

APPENDIX. A.

ACCOUNT OF RAID
carried out on the night of the 22/23rd May 1918 by No 1 Company, 2nd. Battalion Coldstream Guards.

Map Ref: Sheet 57^D.N.E.

A raid was carried out on the enemy lines at F.12.a.5.8. at 12.30 a.m. The party consisted of 2/Lieut: G.C.L. ATKINSON, and 35 O.R's, all volunteers. The party formed up on a tape just outside the Orchard at F.11.b.8.8, after passing through gaps cut in our wire. They were in position at 12.25 a.m. At Zero, the barrage opened and the party immediately xxxxxx closed up to the barrage, and rushed into the enemy's line as soon as the barrage lifted.

Two men were seen to leave the trench and are believed to have been shot. The Light Machine Gun in the post fired about 25 rounds which did no harm. The man firing the Light Machine Gun and the gun, were captured, the recall signal given, and the whole party were back in our trenches with the prisoner and the Light Machine Gun within 10 minutes from Zero.

The artillery arrangements were excellent, and the barrage scheme worked without a hitch.

4 O.R's were slightly wounded through keeping close to our own barrage.

No casualties were inflicted by the enemy's fire.

Lieut: Colonel,
Commanding,
2nd. Battalion Coldstream Guards.

1st June 1918.

WAR DIARY
INTELLIGENCE SUMMARY

(Erase heading not required.)

Army Form C. 2118.

Place	Date	Hour	Summary of Events and Information	Remarks and references to Appendices
In-the-field.	June 1st.		Front Line Trenches. AVELUY. (Casualties 2 O.R's Killed. 6 O.R's Wounded).	
	2nd.		-do- 2/Lieuts: F.J.P.CHITTY, F.D.BISSEKER, G.C.BRASSEY, A.L.MARTIN, M.C., D.C.M., and Draft of 23 O.R's joined the Battalion.	
	3rd.		-do- The Battalion was relieved by the 1st Battalion Irish Guards, and marched back to trenches near MONCHY becoming the Battalion in Reserve. (Casualties. 1 O.R. Killed & 1 O.R. Wounded).	
	4th.		MONCHY Trenches. (Reserve).	
	5th.		-do-	
	6th.		-do- The Battalion was relieved about 7 p.m. by the 2nd Battalion South Staffordshire Regiment and entrained to SAULTY, billets being taken over in the Chateau Grounds. (Casualty 1 O.R. Wounded).	
	7th.		SAULTY (Training). Draft of 4 O.R's joined the Battalion.	
	8th.		-do-	
	9th.		-do- 2/Lt: G.C.L.ATKINSON was awarded the M.C. for services in connection with the Raid of the 22/23rd May 1918.	
	10th.		-do- Draft of 4 O.R's joined the Battalion.	
	11th.		-do- Lieut: O.P.BLACKER, M.C., joined the Battalion from the 4th Battn: Coldstream Guards. Notification was read of the grant of the M.C., to Capt: & Q.M./W.T.BROTHERTON, for distinguished service in connection with military operations in France.	
	12th.		-do-	
	13th.		-do- (continued).	

Army Form C. 2118.

WAR DIARY
~~INTELLIGENCE~~ SUMMARY.

(Erase heading not required.)

Instructions regarding War Diaries and Intelligence Summaries are contained in F. S. Regs., Part II. and the Staff Manual respectively. Title pages will be prepared in manuscript.

Place	Date	Hour	Summary of Events and Information	Remarks and references to Appendices
In-the-Field.	June 14th.		SAULTY (Training). Lieut: G.F.B.HADLEY, M.C., 2/Lieuts: E.G.St.C.CHANCE and C.B.GRABURN, and Draft of 10 O.R's joined the Battalion.	
	15th.		—do—	
	16th.		—do—	
	17th.		—do—	
	18th.		—do—	
	19th.		—do—	
	20th.		—do—	
	21st.		—do—	
	22nd.		—do—	
	23rd.		—do—	
	24th.		—do—	
	25th.		—do—	
	26th.		—do— Draft of 11 O.R's joined the Battalion.	
	27th.		—do—	
	28th.		—do— Captain H.J.R.BRIERLY, M.O., proceeded to ENGLAND on a six months tour of duty.	
	29th.		—do—	
	30th.		—do—	

Lieut: Colonel,
Commanding,
2nd. Battalion Coldstream Guards.

WAR DIARY
INTELLIGENCE SUMMARY

(Erase heading not required.)

Army Form C. 2118.

July, 1916

2nd Coldstream Guards

Vol 46

Place	Date	Hour	Summary of Events and Information	Remarks and references to Appendices
In-the-Field.	July 1st.		SAULTY. (Training).	
	2nd.		—do—	
	3rd.		—do—	
	4th.		—do—	
	5th.		The Battalion paraded at 8 p.m. embussed at LARBRET, and relieved the 1st. Battalion Dorset Regiment in the Front Line Trenches of the Centre Brigade Sector.	
	6th.		Front Line Trenches. (HAMELINCOURT). (Casualties. 2 Wounded. Remained at duty).	
	7th.		—do— (Casualties 2 Wounded one of which Remained at duty).	
	8th.		—do— (Casualty. 1 Wounded).	
	9th.		—do— (Casualty. 1 Wounded. Remained at duty).	
	10th.		—do—	
	11th.		—do— The Battalion was relieved about 10 p.m. by the 1st Bn: Irish Guards and marched back to Trenches at RANSART, becoming the Battalion in Reserve.	
	12th.		RANSART Trenches (Reserve).	
	13th.		—do—	
	14th.		—do—	
	15th.		—do—	
	16th.		—do— (continued).	

Army Form C. 2118.

WAR DIARY
~~INTELLIGENCE SUMMARY~~

(Erase heading not required.)

Instructions regarding War Diaries and Intelligence Summaries are contained in F.S. Regs., Part II. and the Staff Manual respectively. Title pages will be prepared in manuscript.

Place	Date	Hour	Summary of Events and Information	Remarks and references to Appendices
In-the-Field.	July 17th.		RANSART Trenches (Reserve). The Battalion paraded at 10.15 p.m. and relieved the 2nd. Battalion Grenadier Guards in the SUPPORT Trenches near HENDECOURT.	
	18th.		SUPPORT Trenches (HENDECOURT).	
	19th.		--do--	
	20th.		--do-- (Casualty. 1 Wounded. Remained at duty). Draft of 7 O.R's joined the Battalion.	
	21st.		--do-- (Casualties. 2 Wounded. Remained at duty). Lieut: E.F.LUTYENS joined the Battalion. (Cas: 1 O.R. Wd. Gas)	
	22nd.		--do-- (Casualties 6 Wounded. Gas).	
	23rd.		--do-- The Battalion paraded at 10 p.m. and relieved the 2nd. Battalion Grenadier Guards in the Front Line Trenches. (Cas: 1 O.R. Wd. Gas)	
	24th.		Front Line Trenches (HAMELINCOURT). (Casualty. 1 Killed. 1 O.R. Wd. Gas).	
	25th.		--do-- (Casualty. 1 O.R. Wounded. Gas)	
	26th.		--do--	
	27th.		--do--	
	28th.		--do-- (Casualties. 2 O.R's Killed. 1 O.R. Wounded). (1 O.R.Wounded. Gas.)	
	29th.		--do-- The Battalion was relieved about 10.30 p.m. by the 1st Bn: Irish Guards and marched back to Trenches at RANSART, becoming the Battalion in Reserve. (Cas: 1 O.R. Wounded).Draft of 4 O.R's joined the Battalion.	
	30th.		RANSART Trenches. (Reserve).	
	31st.		--do-- (Casualties 11 O.R's Wounded).	

[signature] Lient-Colonel,
Commanding.
2nd Battalion Coldstream Guards.

WAR DIARY
or
INTELLIGENCE SUMMARY

(Erase heading not required.)

Army Form C. 2118.

August, 1917.

Place	Date	Hour	Summary of Events and Information	Remarks and references to Appendices
In-the-Field.	August 1st.		RANSART Trenches (Reserve). Casualties 1 O.R. Killed, 2 O.R's Wounded.	
	2nd.		-do-	
	3rd.		-do-	
	4th.		-do- The Battalion paraded about 10 p.m. and relieved the 2nd. Battalion Grenadier Guards in the SUPPORT position (HENDECOURT). Cas: 5 O.R's Wounded.	
	5th.		SUPPORT Position (HENDECOURT). Casualties 1 O.R.Wounded.	
	6th.		-do-	
	7th.		-do-	
	8th.		-do-	
	9th.		-do-	
	10th.		-do- The Battalion paraded at 10 p.m. and relieved the 2nd. Battalion Grenadier Guards in the Front Line Trenches near HAMELINCOURT.	
	11th.		Front Line Trenches (HAMELINCOURT). Casualties. 1 Wounded.	
	12th.		-do- Casualty:- 2/Lt: W.JACKSON, Wounded (Remained at duty).	
	13th.		-do-	
	14th.		-do- Casualties:- 4 Wounded (Gassed).	
	15th.		-do- Casualties :- 1 O.R. Killed & 1 O.B. Wounded.	
	16th.		-do- The Battalion were relieved about 10.30 p.m. by the 1st Battalion Irish Guards and marched back to the Reserve Trenches at RANSART. Cas:- 2 O.R's Wounded.	

Army Form C. 2118.

WAR DIARY
INTELLIGENCE SUMMARY.
(Erase heading not required.)

Instructions regarding War Diaries and Intelligence Summaries are contained in F.S. Regs., Part II. and the Staff Manual respectively. Title pages will be prepared in manuscript.

Place	Date	Hour	Summary of Events and Information	Remarks and references to Appendices
In-the-Field.	Augst. 17th.		RANSART Trenches (Reserve).	
	18th.		-do- The Battalion paraded at 9.30 p.m. and proceeded to the SUPPORT Trenches round ADINFER.	
	19th.		SUPPORT Trenches round ADINFER.	
	20th.		-do- The Battalion paraded at 8.30 p.m. and proceeded by march route to dug-outs at HENDECOURT becoming Battalion in Reserve.	
	21st.		HENDECOURT. (Reserve).	
	22nd.		-do- Casualties :- 3 O.R's Wounded & 1 O.R.Wounded (Remained at duty).	
	23rd.		-do- The Battalion paraded at 7 p.m. and proceeded by march route to Trenches in front of BOIRY remaining as Reserve Battalion. Casualties :- 2 O.R's Wounded (Gassed) Lieut: J.A.ANDERSON, M.C. proceeded to ENGLAND on 6 months tour of duty).	
	24th.		Trenches near BOIRY. (Reserve)	
	25th.		-do- The Battalion paraded at 4 p.m. and relieved the 1st Bn: Welsh Guards in the Front Line Trenches (St. LEGER)	
	26th.		Front Line Trenches. (St.LEGER). (Casualties:- 2 O.R's Killed, 2 O.R's Wounded & 1 O.R. Wounded (Gas).	
	27th.		-do- At 7 a.m. the Battalion attacked. A detailed account of the operations is attached as APPENDIX "A". Casualties :- Capt: E.J.WATSON SMITH, Lieut: G.F.B.HANDLEY, M.B., & 2/Lt: G.O.BRASSEY, KILLED. Capt: L.W.G.ECCLES,M.C. Lieut: E.F.LUTYENS, Lieut: O.E.ESPIN, Lieut: H.M.D.BARLOW, 2/Lt: G.C.L. ATKINSON,M.C., 2/Lt: E.F.S.GRAHAM, & 2/Lt: W.JACKSON, WOUNDED. Draft of 125 O.R's joined the Battalion. Casualties of Other Ranks :- 55 Killed., 57 Missing., 6 Wounded & Missing., 192 Wounded & 4 Wounded (Remained at duty).	APPENDIX "A".
	28th.		The Battalion followed up the German Retirement and consolidated their positions, being relieved by the 8th Bn: King's Own Lancaster Regiment at 11 p.m., and marched back to Trenches near HAMELINCOURT. Casualties :- 1 O.R. Killed & 3 O.R's Wounded.	

(continued).

On 27th August, 1918.   Appendix A.   Reference Sheet 57 C. N.W.

Account of attack made by the 2nd Battalion Coldstream Guards on the 27th August, 1918.

Map reference :-
FRANCE SHEET 57 C. N.W.

The Battalion was ordered to attack on a 1500 yards front in conjunction with the 2nd Bn. Grenadier Guards on the right; the 1st Battn: Irish Guards being in Reserve. The Battalion attacked with

No. 4 Company (Lieut: C.E. Espin) in front.
No. 2 Company (Capt: L.W.G. Eccles, M.C.) left support.
No. 3 Company (Lieut: G.F.B. Handley, M.C.) right support.
No. 1 Company (Capt: E.J. Watson-Smyth) reserve.

The Division on the left did not attack.

Zero hour was at 7-00a.m. it was therefore necessary to form up under cover owing to the daylight.

The Battalion formed up as follows:-

Right half No. 4 Company with No. 3 Company in support in sunken road from B.4.d.4.0. to Crucifix.
Left half No. 4 Company with No.2 Company in support in St. LEGER Wood B.4.b.5.5. to T.28.d.8.8.
No. 1 Company in reserve West of the ridge in B.4.a & c.

As soon as the barrage came down at Zero, No. 4 Company advanced behind it followed by the support Companies at 200 yards distance. No. 1 Company in reserve 400 yards behind support. On the right No. 4 Company got forward a certain distance but the enemy machine guns in Banks Trench in B.5.d. soon opened a withering fire and the right Platoons of No. 3 Company were unable to get out more than 200 yards from the jumping off position. Lieut: G.F.B. Handley and 2nd Lieut: G.C.Brassey were killed here.

In the centre No. 4 Company and the right of No. 2 Company got to the crest line in T.29.d. Here they came under intense M.G. fire from the right flank and were unable to get farther. Before reaching this point Captain L.W.G. Eccles, M.C. and Lieut: H.M.D. Barlow were wounded.

On the extreme left No. 4 Company and No. 2 Company continued to go forward taking many prisoners in the sunk roads in T.29.d. and T.30.c. and got over to Bunhill Trench in T.30.a. and d., Some of No. 4 Company going further than this. The two Platoons of No. 3 Company under Lieut: H.W. Lake dug in in Bunhill Trench under heavy machine gun fire from T.24. and from U.25.a. & b.

Left half of No. 1 Company then came up to the sunken road in T.30.c.. By this time the centre had suffered very severely; all the Officers were hit; and the machine guns fire from the copse in B.6.a. and from B.5.a. and d. was intense. The right was unable to get forward at all.

The Germans kept moving up more machine guns into the banks in T.30. and B.5.b. The centre was therefore withdrawn to LEGER Reserve. On the left the position was very critical; the machine gun fire from all flanks was intense and large bodies of enemy were seen to be moving along the light railway from T.24 central to T.27.d. completely outflanking the party in Bunhill Trench whose numbers had now been reduced by casualties to 18 under Lieut: H.W. Lake. The party of No. 1 Company under Lieut: T.T. Barnard in the sunk road at T.30.c. were also being outflanked from both flanks. It was therefore decided to withdraw and the left was withdrawn to LEGER Reserve. By this time there were about 140 men left in the Battalion. The Battalion therefore took up a position in LEGER Reserve from T.28.b.5.6. to T.29.d.7.0. A Company of 1st Irish Guards taking over the rest of LEGER Reserve to where it joins Banks Trench. Banks Trench was still held by the enemy and our right which had never been able to get forward dug in to cover the right flank assisted by a Company of 1st Irish Guards.

continued:-

Sheet. 2.

The operation was a difficult one for the following reasons :-

(a) Owing to Zero hour for the Brigade on our left being altered to 3 hours later than the Zero hour arranged for this Brigade, our left flank was exposed.
 CROISILLES and the vicinity was strongly occupied with enemy machine guns which covered the ground over which our left advanced.
(b) Banks trench on the right flank was strongly held by the enemy, and was not touched by the creeping barrage.
 The right of the attack came under heavy Machine gunfire at close range from this trench as soon as the advance began; the advance was held up on this flank.
(c) The jumping off place was awkward, particularly on the left. The thick undergrowth of ST.LEGER Wood made it difficult to keep touch and to keep up to the creeping barrage, which moved forward 100 yards in 2 minutes.
(d) The frontage of the Battalion (1,500 yards), necessitated a very wide extension. The enemy was in considerable strength on the ground, and employed a large number of machine guns.

About 7 p.m. the Artillery put down a 10 minutes barrage on Banks Trench in B.4.d; immediately it lifted Irish Guards and our men on the right, rushed in, and the occupants surrendered (1 Officer, 95 Other Ranks and several Machine guns).

The casualties during the operations were as follows :-

Capt: R.J.Watson-Smyth.
Lieut: G.F.B.Handley, M.C.) KILLED.
2/Lieut: G.C.Brassey.

Captain L.W.G.Eccles, M.C.
Lieut: H.M.D.Barlow.
Lieut: B.F.S.Graham.
Lieut: C.B.Espin.   ) WOUNDED.
Lieut: E.F.Lutyens.
2/Lieut: W.Jackson.
2/Lieut: G.C.L.Atkinson, M.C.

and 324 Other Ranks casualties.

-:-:-:-:-:-:-:-:-:-:-:-:-:-:-:-:-:-:-

Army Form C. 2118.

WAR DIARY
or
INTELLIGENCE SUMMARY.
(Erase heading not required.)

Place	Date	Hour	Summary of Events and Information	Remarks and references to Appendices
In the Field.	Augst. 29th.		Trenches near HAMELINCOURT.	
	30th.		BILLY'S BANK, near ADINFER. The Battalion paraded at 2.50 p.m. and marched back to dug-outs in Sunken road called BILLY'S BANK near ADINFER.	
	31st.		-do- A Draft of 5 O.R's joined the Battalion.	
6th September 1918.				

E.M.W.
Lieut: Colonel,
Commanding,
2nd. Battalion Coldstream Guards.

WAR DIARY of 1st Guards September 1918 1 Bn Coldstream Guards

INTELLIGENCE SUMMARY

Army Form C. 2118.

(Erase heading not required).

Instructions regarding War Diaries and Intelligence Summaries are contained in F.S. Regs., Part II and the Staff Manual respectively. Title pages will be prepared in manuscript.

Place	Date	Hour	Summary of Events and Information	Remarks and references to Appendices
In-the-Field.	Septr. 1st.		Capt: A.BRIGGS., Lieut: H.C. HAYES, M.C., Lieut: A.N. HOWARD., Lieut: G. STUBBLY., Lieut: W.C. BUTLER., Lieut: M.W.J. BIDDULPH., 2/Lieut: J.W.C. LINE., 2/Lieut: O.D. FOSTER., 2/Lieut: O.R.P. POLHILL -WRABLE., 2/Lieut: E.V.D.D. JONES and Draft of 179 O.R's from 3rd Bn: Coldstream Guards & 2 O.R's from Base joined the Battalion. The Battalion paraded at 2 p.m. and proceeded to trenches near HAMELINCOURT.	
BILLY'S BANK near ADINFER.				
-do-	2nd.			
Trenches near HAMELINCOURT.	3rd.		The Battalion paraded at 11 a.m. and marched to Valley East of St. LEGER, parading again at 4.40 p.m. and marching to trenches West of LAGNICOURT, arriving at 6 p.m.	
Trenches near LAGNICOURT.	4th.			
-do-	5th.			
-do-	6th.		A Draft of 2 O.R's joined the Battalion.	
-do-	7th.		The Battalion paraded at 6.45 p.m. and relieved the 1st Bn: Coldstream Guards in the SUPPORT Sector, near LOUVERVAL.	
SUPPORT Trenches, (LOUVERVAL).	8th.		2/Lieut: J.B. BECK & 1 O.R. joined the Battalion.	
-do-	9th.			
-do-	10th.			
-do-	11th.		The Battalion was relieved by the 1st Bn: Welsh Guards and marched back to trenches and dug-outs in Valley East of LAGNICOURT.	
Trenches near LAGNICOURT.	12th.		Casualties:- 1 O.R. Wounded (accidental).	
-do-	13th.		Lieut: J.B. SUMNER & 2 O.R's joined the Battalion. continued.	

Army Form C. 2118.

WAR DIARY
INTELLIGENCE SUMMARY.
(Erase heading not required.)

Instructions regarding War Diaries and Intelligence Summaries are contained in F. S. Regs., Part II. and the Staff Manual respectively. Title pages will be prepared in manuscript.

Place	Date	Hour	Summary of Events and Information	Remarks and references to Appendices
In-the-Field	Septr. 14th.			
Trenches near LAGNICOURT.	15th.		The Battalion paraded at 4.30 p.m. and marched back to trenches vacated by the 1st Bn: Coldstream Guards near NOREUIL. A Draft of 2 O.R's joined the Battalion. Casualties:- 1 O.R. Killed & 3 O.R's Wounded by aeroplane bomb.	
Trenches near NOREUIL.	16th.		A Draft of 3 O.R's joined the Battalion.	
	17th.		The Battalion paraded at 7 p.m. and relieved the 1st Bn: Welsh Guards in the FRONT LINE of the Left Brigade Sector. Captain T.D.SPENCER., Lieut: L.O.M.GIBBS & 7 O.R's joined the Battn.	
Front Line trenches (South of MOEUVRES).	18th.		Cas:- 10 O.R's Wounded & 8 O.R's Wounded (Gas).	
	19th.		Lieut: R.V.MARTYN., 2/Lieut: V.W.EARDLEY-BEECHAM & 4 O.R's joined the Battalion. Casualties:- 4 O.R's Wounded & 1 O.R. Wounded (Gas).	
	20th.		Casualties:- 1 O.R. Wounded, 7 O.R's Wounded (Gas) & 1 O.R. Wounded (Remained at duty).	
	21st.		Casualties:- 1 Killed, 4 O.R's Wounded., 7 O.R's Wounded (Gas), & 2 O.R's Wounded (Remained at duty).	
	22nd.		The Battalion was relieved about midnight by parties of the 1st Bn: Welsh Guards, 1st Bn: Irish Guards and 6th Bn: Highland Light Infantry, and marched back to trenches N.E. of LAGNICOURT. A Draft of 6 O.R's joined the Battalion.	
Trenches near LAGNICOURT.	23rd.			
	24th.		A Draft of 1 O.R. joined the Battalion.	

continued.

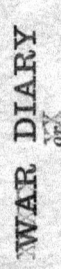

Army Form C. 2118.

WAR DIARY
or
INTELLIGENCE SUMMARY.
(Erase heading not required.)

Place	Date	Hour	Summary of Events and Information	Remarks and references to Appendices
In-the-Field.	Septr. 25th.		Trenches near LONGUEAU. 2/Lieut: W.M.GOODENOUGH joined the Battalion. The following O.R's were awarded the MILITARY MEDAL in connection with the operations of 27th August 1918:-	
			8490 Pte WAKLEY. H. attd. Hd.Qrs., 1st Guards Brigade.	
			17762 Pte(D/Cpl) BURKE. A. P7435 Pte CORK. R.	
			13132 " " CREESE. J. 13601 " BRIAN. G.	
			17815 " " DENT. R.B. 22210 " WHARTON. J.W.	
			5311 " " RICHARDSON. R. 13190 " READ. W.	
			16577 Cpl(L/S) STERN. W. 20125 " RICHMOND. J.	
			17252 " " HEAP. T. 15949 " NICHOLLS. I.	
			21955 Pte MILLS. C.B. 17910 " COUZENS. F.	
			16353 " ADAMS. R.T. 18594 " BATHO. C.M.	
			11740 " COOK. F.C. 12987 " PENNY. S.	
	26th.		—do—	
	27th.		—do— The Battalion paraded at 1.30 a.m. and marched to the Assembly Area near LOUVERVAL, and took part in the attack on the former Hindenburg Line in conjunction with the 2nd. Bn: Grenadier Guards and 1st Bn: Irish Guards. A detailed account of the operations is attached. Ccs:-	APPENDIX "A"
			2/Lieut: E.G.St.G.CHANCE. KILLED.	
			Capt: C.P.BLACKER, M.C. }	
			Lieut: C.J.B.SYKES, M.C. } WOUNDED.	
			Lieut: L.W.J.BIDDULPH. }	
			Lieut: E.CURRIE. }	
			Capt: C.S.WHITTHORPE, M.C. } WOUNDED (at duty).	
			Lieut: A.D.CROSS. }	
			6 O.R's Killed., 11 O.R's Missing & 58 O.R's Wounded.	
	28th. 29th. 30th.		The Battalion withdrew from the positions near GRAINCOURT. Trenches near DEMICOURT. —do—	
	1st October 1918.		6 O.R's wounded. Withdrew at 10 a.m. to trenches near DEMICOURT.	

Lieut-Colonel,
Commanding.,
2nd Battalion Coldstream Guards.

APPENDIX "A"

2nd. Battalion Coldstream Guards.

Map reference:- SHEET 57^C.N.E.

NARRATIVE OF OPERATIONS ON 27.9.1918.

The Battalion left the Assembly area in J.6. & J.12 at 4.50 a.m., 27.9.1918 and proceeded down the MOEUVRE-DEMICOURT Road, thence along SUNKEN ROAD past TROUT POST in K.7.c., to about K.8.central, when it turned due EAST. A hostile barrage was put down from Divisional boundary (Right) due North, and was in depth to the East of the Canal. As casualties were being inflicted, the Battalion occupied the trench running due South from about J.8.d.7.7. Previous to reaching this trench Battalion Headquarters received two direct hits, wounding Lieut: C.J.B. SYMON, M.C., and Lieut: G.STUBLEY, and several Other Ranks and killing Company Sergeant Major E.IRVING,D.C.M., and 2 Other Ranks. This occurred at 6.10 a.m. 10 minutes later the Battalion advanced - Companies in succession, each in artillery formation, and reached the East side of the CANAL, suffering 20 further casualties. The Battalion then moved up GREY TRENCH near the entrance to which 2/Lieut: E.G.St.G. CHANCE was killed and Captain C.S.NELTHORPE, M.C., and Captain C.P.BLACKER, M.C. were hit. The Battalion then relieved the 2nd. Battalion Grenadier Guards who advanced towards the BROWN DOTTED LINE, and took up a position as follows:- Two companies (1 & 2) along SUMMER LANE and two companies (3 & 4) along the trench from K.10.d.4.8. to K.10.b.3.3. On the LEFT was a Company of 2nd. Battalion SCOTS GUARDS who later on moved further up. No 3 Company then extended along the trench to the left to obtain touch on that flank, and on approaching the junction of HUGHES AND STOCK TRENCHES (K.10.b.3.3) was attacked by bomb and machine-gun fire, the latter being very active and firing in the direction of SUMMER LANE. O.C, Commanding No 3 Company, Lieut: A.H.HOWARD, organised a bombing party under Lieut: J.W.S.LANE, who drove the enemy back to K.10.b.4.2. in STOCK TRENCH. Later, the Brigade on the Battalions left attacked and cleared the ground due West of GRAINCOURT, whereupon O.C., No 3 Company sent another party round by the SOUTH & EAST of the Germans who then surrendered - 5 Officers & 50 Other Ranks. In the meantime, Nos 1 & 2 Companies had pushed out 3 Lewis Guns on the ridge, EAST of SUMMER LANE - No 1 Company having two men hit in establishing these posts. No 2 Company's LEWIS GUNS made good practice on the enemy as they retired from the vicinity of CAT TRENCH to GRAINCOURT causing many casualties. The Battalion spent the night in this position and withdrew at 10 a.m. on the 28th. During the operations the following casualties occurred :-

	KILLED.	MISSING.	WOUNDED.	WOUNDED (at duty).
Officers.	1.	-	4.	2.
O.R's.	6.	11.	38.	-

During the above operations the Battalion was commanded by Major. J. BULLOUGH.

Company Commanders :- No 1 Coy..... Captain C.P.BLACKER, M.C.
                               No 2 Coy..... Captain A.BRIGGS.
                               No 3 Coy..... Lieut: A.H.HOWARD.
                               No 4 Coy..... Captain C.S.NELTHORPE, M.C.

Lieut:Colonel,
Commanding,
2nd. Battalion Coldstream Guards.

1st October 1918.

1st Gds. Bde. Gds. Div.

War Diary.

2nd Bn Coldstream Guards.

October 1918.

Army Form C. 2118

WAR DIARY
or
INTELLIGENCE SUMMARY.

2 N'humber Fus / 7CC

Instructions regarding War Diaries and Intelligence Summaries are contained in F.S. Regs., Part II. and the Staff Manual respectively. Title pages will be prepared in manuscript.

Place	Date	Hour	Summary of Events and Information	Remarks and references to Appendices
In-the-Field.	Octr. 1st.		Trenches near DEMICOURT. A Draft of 2 O.R's joined the Battalion.	
	2nd.		-do- The following were awarded decorations in connection with the operations of 27.8.1918.:— **BAR TO THE MILITARY MEDAL.** No. 9991 Pte Charlton (D.C.M.). **MILITARY MEDAL.** No.18221 Pte Dolman. J.F.H. Casualties:— 1 O.R. Wounded (accidental).	
	3rd.		-do-	
	4th.		-do-	
	5th.		-do-	
	6th.		-do-	
	7th.		-do-. The Battalion paraded at 5 p.m. and proceeded by march route to trenches near RIBECOURT, vacated by the Northumberland Fusiliers, 9th Infantry Brigade.	
	8th.		Trenches near RIBECOURT. The Battalion paraded at 10.30 a.m., and proceeded to trenches running North-West of MON PLAISIR FARM, near MASNIERES.	
	9th.		Trenches near MASNIERES. The Battalion attacked at 1.70 a.m. and marched to trenches West of SERANVILLERS. The Battalion attacked at 4.30 a.m. and finally consolidated near CATTENIERES. Casualties :— Lieut: G.R.M.CALDWELL – KILLED. 3 O.R's Killed., 4 O.R's Wounded and 2 O.R's Wounded (Remained at duty).	APPENDIX "A"
	10th.		Trenches near CATTENIERES. The Irish Guards passed through the Battalion and advanced through BEVILLERS to the South-West of QUIEVY, the Battalion following up in SUPPORT and occupying a line North-East of BEVILLERS. At night the Irish Guards continued their advance round QUIEVY, the Battalion then occupying the positions vacated by them South-West of QUIEVY. Casualties :— 1 O.R. Killed, and 7 O.R's Wounded.	

continued:—

Army Form C. 2118.

WAR DIARY
or
INTELLIGENCE SUMMARY

(Erase heading not required.)

Instructions regarding War Diaries and Intelligence Summaries are contained in F. S. Regs., Part II. and the Staff Manual respectively. Title pages will be prepared in manuscript.

Place	Date	Hour	Summary of Events and Information	Remarks and references to Appendices
In the Field.	Oct. 11th.		Trenches South-West of QUIEV X. The Battalion paraded at 1.10 a.m. and moved to billets in QUIEV X. A draft of 5 O.R's joined the Battalion.	
	12th.		QUIEV X. The Battalion paraded at 5.15 p.m. and relieved the 1st Battalion Grenadier Guards in the Front line trenches South-West of SOLESMES. Casualties:- 1 O.R. Wounded.	
	13th.		Front line Trenches (SOLESMES).	
	14th.		—do— Casualties:- 2 O.R's Wounded and 2 O.R's Wounded (Remained at duty).	
	15th.		—do— Casualties:- Capt: C.S.NETTHORPE, M.C. WOUNDED. 3 O.R's Wounded and 2 O.R's Wounded (Remained at duty).	
	16th.		—do— The Battalion was relieved about 7 p.m. by the Duke of Wellington's Regiment, 62nd Division, and marched back to billets in ST. HILAIRE. Casualties:- 1 O.R. Wounded.	
	17th.		ST. HILAIRE. 2/Lieut: H.N.VINCENT & Lieut: L.W.G.ECCLES, M.C., joined the Battalion, also a draft of 3 O.R's.	
	18th.		—do— The undermentioned were awarded decorations in connection with the Operations of 27.8.1918. BAR TO THE MILITARY CROSS. Capt: P.H.WELLS, M.C. R.A.M.C. THE MILITARY CROSS. Lieut: H.W.LAKE. Lieut: C.E.ESPIN. Lieut: T.T.BARNARD. Lieut: C.S.FAREY. att.d Signal Coy. BAR TO THE DISTINGUISHED CONDUCT MEDAL. 8491 Pte E.A.WHITING, D.C.M.,M.M. THE DISTINGUISHED CONDUCT MEDAL. 6554 Cpl.(L/S) H.WHITTAKER. 16109 Cpl(L/S) D.WORRALL. 11992 Pte (L/C) W.HURST. continued:-	

Army Form C. 2118.

WAR DIARY
or
INTELLIGENCE SUMMARY
(Erase heading not required.)

Instructions regarding War Diaries and Intelligence Summaries are contained in F. S. Regs., Part II. and the Staff Manual respectively. Title pages will be prepared in manuscript.

Place	Date	Hour	Summary of Events and Information	Remarks and references to Appendices
In the Field	Oct. 18th.		continued:— The undermentioned were awarded decorations in connection with the Operations of 27.9.1918. THE MILITARY MEDAL. 6076 Sgt. C.WHITE. 19387 Pte(L/C) J.T.DANSON. 11710 Sgt. S.V.LENTELL. 20798 Pte(L/C) A.J.SADLER. 19686 Pte. W.JEPSON. 13733 Pte. A.BENTLEY. 18065 Pte. H.CROWE. 6445 Pte. A.T.RIDOUT. 20356 Pte. J.BALL. 17035 Pte. J.C.GRIMMER, attd 1st. Gds. Bde. T.M.Battery.	APPENDIX "B".
	19th.		ST. HILAIRE. The Battalion paraded at 11.50 p.m. prior to proceeding to the assembly area near ST.P YTHON, prior to attacking the German Lines North of SOLESMIES. 2/Lieut: F.J.P.CHILTY was Classified B.iii and taken off the strength of the Battalion. A draft of 7 O.R's joined the Battalion.	
	20th.		Near ST.P YTHON. The Battalion attacked at 2.40 a.m. the German Lines North of SOLESMIES as Reserve Battalion to the 2nd. Bn. Grenadier Guards and the 1st Bn. Irish Guards. (See Appendix "B"). Casualties:— 5 O.R's Wounded.	
	21st.		ST.P YTHON. The Battalion paraded at 4 p.m. and marched back to billets in ST. HILAIRE. Casualties:— 5 O.R's Wounded.	
	22nd.		ST. HILAIRE. The battalion paraded at 5 p.m. and moved to billets in CARNIERES. A draft of 4 O.R's joined the Battalion. Capt: C.P.BLACKER, M.O. rejoined the Battalion.	
	23rd.		CARNIERES. (Training).	
	24th.		—do—	
	25th.		—do—	
	26th.		—do—	

continued:—

Army Form C. 2118.

WAR DIARY
INTELLIGENCE SUMMARY

Place	Date	Hour	Summary of Events and Information	Remarks and references to Appendices
In-the-Field.	Octr. 27th.		CARNIERES. (Training).	
	28th.		—do— In the men inspected by Major General T.G. MATHESON C.B. Commanding Field Division. The B.N. marched past his General, in column of platoon.	
	29th.		—do—	
	30th.		—do—	
	31st.		—do— A draft of 120 O.R's joined the Battalion, 2/Lieut: H.W.WILD also joined the Battalion. The Battalion paraded at 11.30.a.m. and moved to billets in ST. HILAIRE. A draft of 6 O.R's joined the Battalion.	
1st November 1918.				

M Bullrd
Major,
Commanding,
2nd. Battalion Coldstream Guards.

APPENDIX. "A"

2nd. Battalion Coldstream Guards.

OPERATIONS of 2nd. BATTALION COLDSTREAM GUARDS from 9th – 17th OCTOBER 1918.

Map reference:- SHEET 57B. N.W.

The Battalion marched through MASNIERES on October 8th and it assembled on old German trenches running North & West of MON PLAISIR FARM (G.27.d) where it was bombarded with gas shells, but no casualties were inflicted. The Germans had made a counter-attack with tanks on the 2nd Division during the day, and the situation was rather obscure, as there seemed to be no continuous line. The Battalion was ordered to line up in the trench running West of SERANVILLERS with the 2nd. Battalion Grenadier Guards on its left; the Inter-Battalion boundary running North-East through SERANVILLERS – LA TARGETTE and WAMBAIX. Nos. 2 & 3 Companies were in front (No 2 on the left), No 4 Company in Support, and No 1 Company in Reserve. At Zero hour (4.30 a.m) on the 9th October, the artillery barrage fell on the GREEN LINE, which ran roughly S.E. through LA TARGETTE, and Nos. 2 & 3 Companies immediately left the trench and closed up to the barrage, No 4 Company following 400 yards behind, and No 1 Company following still farther back in reserve. SERANVILLERS and LA TARGETTE were found to be clear of the enemy, but they seemed to be strongly posted in WAMBAIX. The first objective of the Battalion was the BLUE LINE running due East of WAMBAIX from H.10.d.6.5. – H.16.d.6.0. This line was soon occupied, No 2 Company capturing 2 Machine-guns in WAMBAIX. The barrage then lifted and the advance continued East-North-East over the railway through H.18.a & b. The Southern half of CATTENIERES was mopped up and an effort was made to take the GREEN LINE which ran from I.7.d.2.9. to I.13.b.5.6. The Germans, however, were very strongly posted in prepared positions East of BEAUVOIS, and also along the main road running from CAMBRAI to LE CATEAU. While Nos. 2 & 3 Companies were trying to consolidate this line they suffered several casualties and Lieut: G.R.M.CALDWELL was wounded and died from his wound on reaching the Dressing-station. As the Battalion on the left could not get up to the GREEN LINE, orders were given to withdraw to CATTENIERES and the road running South-East through H.12.d. and I.13.a. with the Support and Reserve Companies respectively lining the railway in rear. This line was consolidated and the position remained thus during the night. On the morning of 10th October, the Irish Guards passed through both Battalions, and advanced by bounds through BEVILLERS, with the Battalion following up to each successive bound in support. The enemy only offered small resistance by means of isolated machine-gun posts which were quickly overcome, the last bound of the Irish Guards being South-West of QUIEVY and the Battalion occupying a line North-East of BEVILLERS. During the evening the Irish Guards advanced round QUIEVY, leaving the town to be mopped up next day, and the Battalion moved up to the positions vacated by the Irish Guards South-West of the town.

On the 11th and 12th October, the Battalion rested at QUIEVY, and on the evening of the 12th moved up to relieve the 1st Battalion Grenadier Guards, who had gone through the Irish Guards, in a line running East of FONTAINE-au-TERTRE FARM, with the front line well forward at the railway running South-West of SOLESMES, where they stayed for four days till they were relieved by the 62nd Division.

The casualties during this period were as follows :-

Lieut: G.R.M.CALDWELL.	KILLED.
Capt: C.S.NELTHORPE, M.C.	WOUNDED.
4 Other Ranks.	KILLED.
44 -do-	WOUNDED.
6 -do-	WOUNDED (Remained at duty).

Bullock
Ma
2nd. Battalion Coldst.

APPENDIX. "B".

2nd. Battalion Coldstream Guards.

NARRATIVE OF OPERATIONS ON 20TH OCTOBER 1918.

Reference Map:- 51.C. S.E.

The Guards Division was ordered to capture the high ground North of SOLESMES on the morning of 20.10.1918. The 62nd Division was on the Right and the 19th Division on the Left.

The Guards Division attacked with the 1st Guards Brigade on the Right and the 3rd Guards Brigade on the Left.

The Battalion was in Reserve to the 2nd. Battalion Grenadier Guards on the Right and the 1st Battalion Irish Guards on the Left, and was ordered to form a defensive flank on the Right from W.20.c.6.7. to V.30.d.6.8. This was necessary, because the 62nd Division was ordered to remain on the 1st objective for 5 hours after the Guards Division had captured the 2nd. objective. After the lapse of this period, the 62nd Division was to capture its 2nd objective, joining to and in continuation Southwards from the Guards Division.

The Battalion left billets in ST.HILAIRE at 11.30 p.m., 19.10.1918 and marched to the assembly area in V.28. The night was dark and it was raining hard, which made the move a matter of difficulty. The Battalion reached the assembly area at 1.15 a.m., and moved forward to the attack at 2.40 a.m. in artillery formation. The road running North and South through V.24.central and V.30.b., was reached without much difficulty at 3.30 a.m., each Company having found the bridges across the SELLE without any delay. On reaching this road, No 3 Company encountered 20 Germans who at once surrendered. Nos. 3 & 4 Companies immediately proceeded to form a defensive flank facing S.E. from W.20.c.1.0. to W.25.b.2.5. and from W.25.b.2.5. to V.30.d.6.8. respectively.

No 2 Company advanced to W.19.c. and dug themselves in, in rear of the leading Battalions, and No 1 Company was kept with Battalion Headquarters in the road from V.30.b. to the Cross Roads at V.30.d.6.8. with posts on the high ground in front. Touch was immediately gained with both flanks and the two leading Battalions.

The hostile barrage had all this time been indifferent, but at 8 a.m. very heavy shell fire was opened on the area and continued throughout the day with the utmost persistency, making any movement difficult and runners in particular had a very arduous time. The Battalion remained in the same position till the evening of the 21.10.18 when it was withdrawn, and marched to billets in ST.HILAIRE.

Major,
Commanding,
2nd. Battalion Coldstream Guards.

WAR DIARY or INTELLIGENCE SUMMARY

Army Form C. 2118.

November, 1918.

1st Bn Coldstream Guards Vol 50

Place	Date	Hour	Summary of Events and Information	Remarks and references to Appendices
In-the-Field.	Novr. 1st.		ST. HILAIRE. The Battalion paraded at 4 p.m. and marched to billets in VERTAIN via ST. VAAST and ST. PYTHON.	
	2nd.		VERTAIN. The Battalion paraded at 1.15 p.m. and proceeded by march route to relieve the 24th(S) Bn: Royal Fusiliers & 2nd. Bn: Oxford & Buckinghamshire Light Infantry in the Front Line trench S. Battalion Headquarters being established at RUESNES.	
	3rd.		RUESNES. The Battalion followed up the Retreat of the enemy through VILLERS-POL and assembled N.E. of the village, prior to attacking the German lines.	
	4th.		VILLERS-POL. The Battalion attacked at dawn in conjunction with the 1st Bn: Coldstream Guards on the right, and the 1st Bn: Middlesex Regiment on the left. Casualties:—	APPENDIX "A".
			Lieut: J.C.HAMES, M.C. — KILLED.	
			2/Lieut: H.N.VINCENT. — WOUNDED.	
			2/Lieut: V.W.BARNES ASHBURY. } — WOUNDED.	
			Lieut: J.P.SAUNDERS. — KILLED.	
			Capt: L.W.G.BOOKES, M.C. — WOUNDED (Remained at duty.)	
			6 Other Ranks. — KILLED.	
			73 " " — WOUNDED.	
			4 " " — MISSING.	
			At 9.30 a.m. the Grenadier Guards went through the Battalion and at 1.30 p.m. the Battalion marched back to billets in VILLERS-POL. Lewis: A.M.C. BUTCHER, M.C. and a draft of 2 O.R's joined the Battalion.	
	5th.		VILLERS-POL. The Battalion paraded at 4 p.m. and marched to billets in the Chateau at WARGNIES-LE-PETIT.	
	6th.		WARGNIES-LE-PETIT. Cas: 5 O.R's Killed and 14 O.R's Wounded.	
			continued:—	

Army Form C. 2118.

WAR DIARY
or
INTELLIGENCE SUMMARY.
(Erase heading not required.)

Instructions regarding War Diaries and Intelligence Summaries are contained in F. S. Regs., Part II. and the Staff Manual respectively. Title pages will be prepared in manuscript.

Place	Date	Hour	Summary of Events and Information	Remarks and references to Appendices
In the Field.	Nov. 7th.		WARGNIES-LE-PETIT. The Battalion paraded at 7.15 p.m. and proceeded by march route to billets in BAVAI.	
	8th.		BAVAI. The Battalion paraded at 12 p.m. and followed up the German retirement through MAUBEUGE, and established itself on the outskirts of the fortress. A draft of 5 O.R's joined the Battalion.	
	9th.		MAUBEUGE. Lieut: C.G.HEYWOOD, 2/Lieut: V.B.LONGWORTH and a draft of 99 O.R's joined the Battalion.	
	10th.		-do- Casualty:- 1 O.R. Wounded.	
	11th.		-do- Hostilities ceased at 11 a.m. and in the afternoon the Battalion marched from the outskirts of the Town to billets at MAUBEUGE. The following were awarded decorations in connection with the Operations of the 9th October, 1918:- THE MILITARY CROSS. Major: J.Bullough. Lieut: J.W.S.Lane. Lieut: A.N.Howard. THE MILITARY MEDAL. No.17754 Pte Hammond. L.R. 10876 Sgt Lea. T. 15343 " Goddard. F. 17806 Pte Antell. A. 6045 " Davis. G.A. 15746 " Willer. J. 18748 " Withers. C.	
	12th.		MAUBEUGE. (Training).	
	13th.		-do-	
	14th.		-do-	
	15th.		-do-	

continued:-

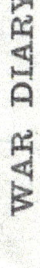

Army Form C. 2118.

WAR DIARY
or
INTELLIGENCE SUMMARY.
(Erase heading not required.)

Instructions regarding War Diaries and Intelligence Summaries are contained in F.S. Regs., Part II. and the Staff Manual respectively. Title pages will be prepared in manuscript.

Place	Date	Hour	Summary of Events and Information	Remarks and references to Appendices
In-the Field.	Nov. 16th.			
MAUBEUGE. (Training).	17th.		The following N.C.O. was awarded the MILITARY MEDAL in connection with the Operations of 9th October 1918:- No.6687 L/C. CLARK. A.	
—do—	18th.		The Battalion paraded at 8 a.m. and commenced the march into Germany as part of the Army of Occupation in accordance with the terms of the Armistice, proceeding via VIEUX RENG and ROUVROI to HAULCHIN, staying the night at the latter village.	
HAULCHIN.	19th.		The Battalion paraded at 7.30 a.m. and continued the march as far as ANDERLUES. Route:- ESTINNE - BINCHE.	
ANDERLUES.	20th.		The Battalion moved to billets in GILLY, CHARLEROI, parading at 8.50 a.m. and marched past the Army Commander in CHARLEROI SQUARE, arriving about 12.30 p.m.	
GILLY, CHARLEROI. (Training).	21st.			
—do—	22nd.			
—do—	23rd.			
—do—	24th.		The Battalion paraded at 9 a.m. and continued the march into Germany starting the night in billets at FOSSE. Route:- CHAMBRE - CHATELET - PRESE.	
FOSSE.	25th.		The Battalion moved on to billets at WEPION parading at 8 a.m. and proceeding via SART ST.LAURENT and BOIS DE VILLERS.	
WEPION. (Training).	26th.			
—do—	27th.			

Continued:-

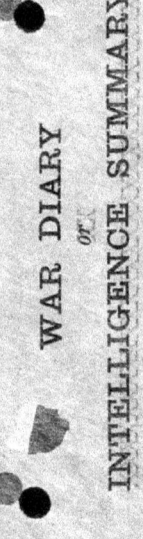

WAR DIARY

INTELLIGENCE SUMMARY

Army Form C. 2118.

Place	Date	Hour	Summary of Events and Information	Remarks and references to Appendices
In-the-Field.	Novr. 28th.		WERLON.	
	29th.		FLORLE. (Training)	
	30th.		-do- -do-	
	1st December 1918.		The Battalion paraded at 9 a.m. and continued its march as far as FLORLE, the route taken being DAVE - MAIRINE Station.	

J.P Murray
Lieut:Colonel,
Commanding,
2nd. Battalion Coldstream Guards.

WAR DIARY or INTELLIGENCE SUMMARY

Army Form C. 2118.

December, 1918

2nd Bn. Coldstream Guards

Place	Date	Hour	Summary of Events and Information	Remarks and references to Appendices
In the Field.	Dec: 1st.		FLOREE. (Training)	
	2nd		—do—	
	3rd		—do—	
	4th		—do—	
	5th		—do— The Battalion paraded at 8-15a.m. and continued the march as far as MAFFE. Route :— FRANCESSE - SOREE - "Pt of MAGNE - EVELETTE - HAVELANGE."	
	6th		MAFFE. The Battalion moved to HEYD, parading at 8-30a.m. and proceeding via GROS CHENE - PETIT HAN - BARVAUX.	
	7th		HEYD. The Battalion paraded at 8-25a.m. and moved to LIERNEUX proceeding via MANHAY - VAUX CHAVANNE and JELIGNE.	
	8th		LIERNEUX. (Training)	
	9th		—do— The following were awarded decorations in connection with the operations of the 4th November, 1918:— BAR TO MILITARY MEDAL. 13225 Gdsn.(L/C) W.H. Coates, M.M. 15941 " " P. Cowle, M.M. THE MILITARY MEDAL. 17567 Sgt. Studd R. 13003 " Shipman E. 17463 Cpl.(L/S) Burrows J. 9243 Gdsn.(L/C) Chisholm,D.C.M. J.W. 18375 " Sharpen W. 17183 " Meekin J. 21431 " Hopkins E.	
	10th		LIERNEUX. (Training).	

Army Form C. 2118.

WAR DIARY
or
INTELLIGENCE SUMMARY.

Instructions regarding War Diaries and Intelligence Summaries are contained in F. S. Regs., Part II. and the Staff Manual respectively. Title pages will be prepared in manuscript.

Place	Date	Hour	Summary of Events and Information	Remarks and references to Appendices
In the Field.	Decr. 11th		LIERNEUX. The Battalion paraded at 9-35a.m. and continued the march into GERMANY, staying the night in billets at RODT (GERMANY). Route :- GORONNE and VEILSAM.	
	12th		RODT. The Battalion crossed the German Frontier at 1-45p.m.	
	13th		BULLINGEN. The Battalion moved to billets at BULLINGEN, parading at 9-15a.m. and proceeding via St. VITH and AMEL.	
	14th		HOLLERATH. The Battalion paraded at 8-30a.m. and continued the march as far as HOLLERATH. Route :- LOSHEIMER and GRABEN.	
	15th		KALL. The Battalion moved on to billets in KALL parading at 8-00a.m., and proceeding via HALLENTHAL - BLUMENTHAL and REIFFERSCHEIT.	
	16th		SCHWERFEN. The Battalion moved to SCHWERFEN parading at 8-00a.m. and proceeding via ROGGENDORF.	
	17th		ERP. The Battalion continued the march as far as ERP parading at 8-5a.m. Route :- ZULPICH.	
	18th		KENDENICH. The Battalion paraded at 8-00a.m. and marched to billets in KENDENICH, proceeding via LIBLAR.	
	19th		BOCKLEMUND. The Battalion paraded at 8-10a.m. and continued its march as far as BOCKLEMUND, the route taken being LIND - MUNG - ESSDORF.	
	20th		-do- (Training).	
	21st		-do- -do-	
	22nd		EHRENFELD. The Battalion paraded at 10a.m. and marched to its final destination at EHRENFELD. Route :- BICKENDORF. (Training).	

Army Form C. 2118.

WAR DIARY
or
INTELLIGENCE SUMMARY

(Erase heading not required.)

Place	Date	Hour	Summary of Events and Information	Remarks and references to Appendices
In the Field.	Decr. 23rd.		EHRENFELD. (Training). Lieut: Viscount H.R. Gage, 2/Lieut: G.R.Forrestier-Walker and 2/Lieut: A.B.C. Reynolds joined the Battalion.	
	24th		-do- (Training).	
	25th.		-do- -do-	
	26th.		-do- -do-	
	27th		-do- -do-	
	28th		-do- -do-	
	29th		-do- -do-	
	30th		-do- -do-	
	31st		-do- -do-	

1st January, 1919.

J.M.Brunty

Lieutenant-Colonel,
Commanding,
2nd Battalion Coldstream Guards.

Army Form C. 2118.

WAR DIARY
or
~~INTELLIGENCE SUMMARY~~ 2nd Bn. Coldstream Gds. January 1919

(Erase heading not required.)

Place	Date	Hour	Summary of Events and Information	Remarks and references to Appendices
In the field.	Jany. 1st	EHRENFELD.	(Training). The following were mentioned in Field Marshall Sir Douglas HAIG'S despatches for conspicuous gallantry in the Field :- Lieut: Colonel E.P.Brassey M.C. Major J.Bullough M.C. Captain. C.P.Blacker M.C. 2/Lieut: G.C.L.Atkinson M.C. No.9543 Sgt A.Kirk. 5112 " G.Osborne M.M.	
	2nd	EHRENFELD.	(Training).	
	3rd	--do--	Lieut: J.D.LEGGE M.C. joined the Battalion.	
	4th	--do--	--do--	
	5th	--do--	2/Lieut: H.O.LUSH and 29 O.R. joined the Battalion.	
	6th	--do--	The Kings' Colour and the Regimental Colour arrived at COLOGNE Station at 10.15a.m. and were escorted to Battalion Headquarters.	
	7th	--do--		
	8th	--do--	8 O.R. joined the Battalion.	
	9th	--do--	The following appeared in the London Gazette dated 31.12.1918. AWARDED THE DISTINGUISHED CONDUCT MEDAL. No. 8864 Sgt J.C. Spence. 8173 " H.E.Gough.	
	10th to 23rd.	--do--		

Army Form C. 2118.

WAR DIARY
or
INTELLIGENCE SUMMARY.

(Erase heading not required.)

Instructions regarding War Diaries and Intelligence Summaries are contained in F. S. Regs., Part II. and the Staff Manual respectively. Title pages will be prepared in manuscript.

Place	Date	Hour	Summary of Events and Information	Remarks and references to Appendices
In the field.	Jany: 24th.		EHRENFELD. (Training). The following Decorations were awarded in connection with the Operations on 4th November, 1918.	
			THE MILITARY CROSS. THE DISTINGUISHED CONDUCT MEDAL.	
			2/Lieut: H.H.Vincent. No.9567 Sgt O.Warner M.M.	
			" C.R.P.Polhill-Drabble.	
			" J.B.Beck.	
			Information was received that the undermentioned have been awarded the MERITORIOUS SERVICE MEDAL.	
			No. 8317 R.Q.M.S. T. Davis M.M.	
			10376 C.Q.M.S. A. Douglas.(1st Battn: late 2nd Battn:)	
	25th to 31st.		EHRENFELD. (Training).	

1st February 1919.

[signature]
Lieut: Colonel,
Commanding,
2nd Battalion Coldstream Guards.

SECRET.   APPENDIX "A".

2nd. Battalion Coldstream Guards.

NARRATIVE OF OPERATIONS from 2.11.18 to 4.11.18.

Reference Map:- SHEET 51 & 51.a.

The Battalion left VERTAIN on the evening of 2.11.1918 and marched to RUESNES, relieving the 2nd Battalion Oxford & Buckinghamshire Light Infantry and the 24th ( ) Royal Fusiliers in the front line. The intention was that the Battalion would attack on the morning of the 4th inst., with the 1st Battalion Coldstream Guards on the right and the 1st Battalion Middlesex Regiment on the left, and capture the BLUE LINE which ran along the road from the QUATRE VENTS to L.35.b.5.9.

During the afternoon of the 3rd inst., it was discovered that the enemy was withdrawing from VILLERS-POL and the Battalion was ordered to advance to the BLUE LINE as speedily as possible.

The advance commenced at 8 p.m. with No 1 Company on the right and No 2 Company on the left; No 4 Company in Support and Nos 3 Company in Reserve. The latter company had to carry 4 infantry bridges and place them over the RHONELLE. Little opposition was met until the centre of VILLERS-POL, where the leading waves came under heavy machine-gun fire. The Battalion advanced to 400 yards West of the BLUE LINE where it dug itself in at 11.30 p.m. XX, the high ground immediately in front being strongly held by the enemy. The 1st Battalion on the right conformed. The advance was continued on the morning of the 4th under a creeping barrage, lifting 100 yards every 3 minutes to the GREEN LINE running from Q.27.d.6.0. to Q.35.d.3.0. The Battalion advanced in the same order as the previous day but the leading company had 3 platoons in the leading wave and 1 platoon in Support. The objective was reached at 7 a.m. but owing to a very heavy mist direction was extremely hard to maintain and the Battalion consolidated slightly South of their allotted positions.

During the last 700 yards of the advance severe fighting took place and very heavy casualties were inflicted on the enemy including several gun teams. The Battalion also captured 200 prisoners and 8 Field-guns, many machine-guns and a few trench mortars. At 9.30 A.M. the Grenadier Guards went through the Battalion and in the evening the Battalion withdrew to billets in VILLERS-POL.

During the operations the following casualties occurred:-

Lieut: J.R.SAUNDERS.	KILLED.
Lieut: J.C.HAYES, M.C.	
2/Lt: H.N.VINCENT.	WOUNDED.
2/Lt: V.W.EARDLEY-BEECHAM.	
Capt: L.W.G.ECCLES, M.C.	WOUNDED (Remained at duty).
5 Other Ranks.	KILLED.
77 -do-	WOUNDED.
3 -do-	MISSING.

6th November 1918.

Lieut:Colonel,
Commanding,
2nd. Battalion Coldstream Gds.

www.ingramcontent.com/pod-product-compliance
Lightning Source LLC
Chambersburg PA
CBHW081405160426
43193CB00013B/2109